SCHOLASTIC

Building Comprehension

Reading Passages With High-Interest Practice Activities

Crosswords, Mazes, Games, and More to Build Skills in Making Inferences, Using Context Clues, Comparing & Contrasting, Identifying Fact & Opinion, and Making Predictions

by Karen Kellaher

New York • Toronto • London • Auckland • Sydney
Mexico City • New Delhi • Hong Kong • Buenos Aires

Teaching Resources

To Anna Caroline, with love and pride:
What an awesome reader you have become!
Thanks for being my in-house adviser.

Cover design by Maria Lilja

Cover and interior illustrations by Teresa Anderko

Interior design by Ellen Matlach for Boultinghouse & Boultinghouse

ISBN-13: 978-0-439-36533-8
ISBN-10: 0-439-36533-3

Published by Scholastic Inc.

Printed in the U.S.A.

6 7 8 9 10 40 14 13 12

Contents

Introduction

For more than a decade, reading comprehension has been the subject of increasing scrutiny. At one level, the attention has centered on the very way we define reading comprehension. Most of us think of comprehension as the process of constructing meaning from text, of making sense of what we read. Researchers Harris and Hodges use such a "constructivist" definition in their *Literacy Dictionary* (1995). They describe reading comprehension as "the construction of the meaning of a written text through a reciprocal interchange of ideas between the reader and the message in a particular text." Laudably, this and similar definitions give center stage to both reader and text. They acknowledge that reading is an active process of *building* meaning rather than the passive *acquisition* of meaning.

However, some researchers argue that reading comprehension is even more complex than the above definition suggests. The RAND group, a panel of reading experts charged by the U.S. Department of Education with the task of creating a national literacy research agenda, broadened the definition to include other factors, including the context in which the reading takes place. They define comprehension as "the process of simultaneously extracting and constructing meaning through interaction and involvement with written language. It consists of three elements: the reader, the text, and the activity or purpose for reading" (RAND Reading Study Group, 2002).

Putting Research Into Practice

Of course, as educators we seek not just to define reading comprehension but to teach it. This too has been a research focus in recent years. The National Reading Panel has pinpointed several effective strategies for boosting comprehension. These include, among others, having students monitor their own understanding as they read (and reread when necessary), having them work cooperatively on a common reading task and participate in group discussion, and having them answer questions about the text (National Reading Panel, 2000).

Another important way to help boost comprehension is to provide both fiction and nonfiction reading materials. Each is organized in a different way and presents the reader with unique demands (RAND Reading Study Group, 2002). For example, with fiction, readers become familiar with basic story structure and use this knowledge to make predictions and draw conclusions about the text. With nonfiction, readers are exposed to main ideas and supporting details. They may be required to use context clues to understand highly technical words.

About This Book

In this book you'll find an array of fiction and nonfiction passages that relate to the interests of third and fourth graders, helping students tap into prior knowledge. Each passage is broken into sections with subtitles to help kids zero in on main ideas. The passages are followed by several engaging comprehension activities that address key points from each passage and help students build comprehension skills.

The questions in these activities were carefully crafted to address six important skills. They include:

- Identifying main ideas and important details
- Predicting
- Making inferences
- Comparing and contrasting
- Identifying fact and opinion
- Using context clues

Practicing these skills together in class helps prepare students to use the skills on their own with other kinds of reading materials, including books, magazine and newspaper articles, and Web sites.

This book also provides a host of other benefits to you and your young readers. The passages and activities are engaging and sure to motivate even the most reluctant readers. They can be used for instant homework or class work. In addition, these reading comprehension activities help students prepare for high-stakes standardized tests—and help you identify where additional instruction or practice may be needed before test time. The activities also help you meet state and national reading standards.

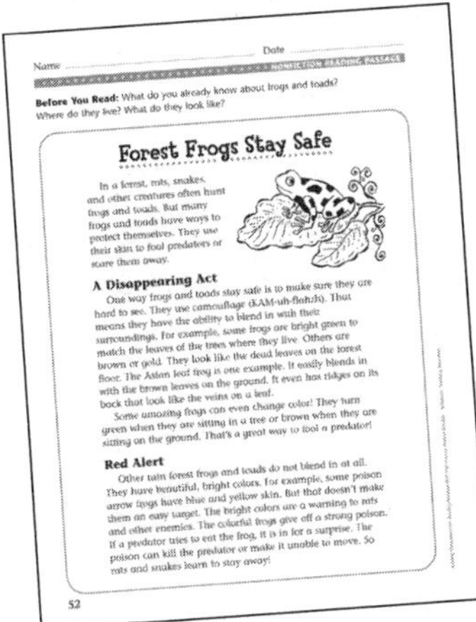

Name .... Date ....

Before You Read: What do you already know about frogs and toads? Where do they live? What do they look like?

Forest Frogs Stay Safe

In a forest, rats, snakes, and other creatures often hunt frogs and toads. But many frogs and toads have ways to protect themselves. They use their skin to fool predators or scare them away.

A Disappearing Act

One way frogs and toads stay safe is to make sure they are hard to see. They use camouflage (KAM-uh-flahzh). That means they have the ability to blend in with their surroundings. For example, some frogs are bright green to match the leaves of the trees where they live. Others are brown or gold. They look like the dead leaves on the forest floor. The Asian leaf frog is one example. It easily blends in with the brown leaves on the ground. It even has ridges on its back that look like the veins on a leaf.

Some amazing frogs can even change color! They turn green when they are sitting in a tree or brown when they are sitting on the ground. That's a great way to fool a predator!

Red Alert

Other rain forest frogs and toads do not blend in at all. They have beautiful, bright colors. For example, some poison arrow frogs have blue and yellow skin. But that doesn't make them an easy target. The bright colors are a warning to rats and other enemies. The colorful frogs give off a strong poison. If a predator tries to eat the frog, it is in for a surprise. The poison can kill the predator or make it unable to move. So rats and snakes learn to stay away!

52

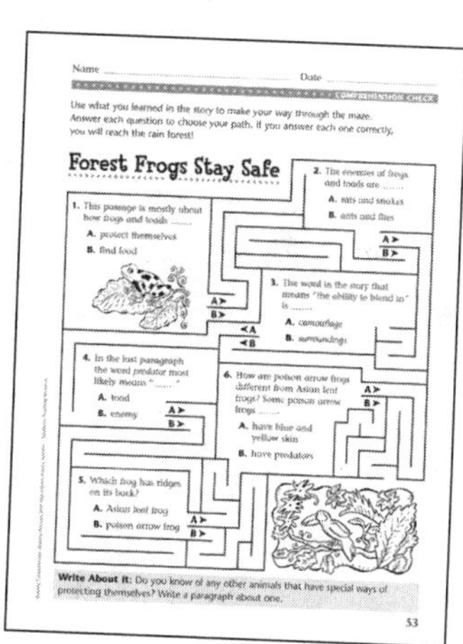

Name .... Date ....

Use what you learned in the story to make your way through the maze. Answer each question to choose your path. If you answer each one correctly, you will reach the rain forest!

Forest Frogs Stay Safe

1. This passage is mostly about how frogs and toads ______.
   A. protect themselves
   B. find food
2. The enemies of frogs and toads are ______.
   A. rats and snakes
   B. ants and flies
3. The word in the story that means "the ability to blend in" is ______.
   A. camouflage
   B. surroundings
4. In the last paragraph the word *predator* most likely means "______."
   A. food
   B. enemy
5. Which frog has ridges on its back?
   A. Asian leaf frog
   B. poison arrow frog
6. How are poison arrow frogs different from Asian leaf frogs? Some poison arrow frogs ______.
   A. have blue and yellow skin
   B. have predators

Write About It: Do you know of any other animals that have special ways of protecting themselves? Write a paragraph about one.

53

Connections to the Standards

The activities in this book connect to the following language arts standards and benchmarks outlined by Mid-continent Research for Education and Learning (McREL), a nationally recognized nonprofit organization that collects and synthesizes national and state K–12 standards.

Uses the general skills and strategies of the reading process.

- Previews text (e.g., skims material; uses pictures, textual clues, and text format).
- Establishes a purpose for reading (e.g., for information, for pleasure, to understand a specific viewpoint).
- Makes, confirms, and revises simple predictions about what will be found in a text (e.g., uses prior knowledge and ideas presented in text, illustrations, titles, topic sentences, key words, and foreshadowing clues).
- Uses phonetic and structural analysis techniques, syntactic structure, and semantic context to decode unknown words (e.g., vowel patterns, complex word families, syllabication, root words, affixes).
- Uses a variety of context clues to decode unknown words (e.g., draws on earlier reading, reads ahead).
- Understands level-appropriate reading vocabulary (e.g., synonyms, antonyms, homophones, multi-meaning words).
- Monitors own reading strategies and makes modifications as needed (e.g., recognizes when he or she is confused by a section of text, questions whether the text makes sense).
- Adjusts speed of reading to suit purpose and difficulty of the material.
- Understands the author's purpose (e.g., to persuade, to inform) or point of view.

Uses reading skills and strategies to understand and interpret a variety of literary texts.

- Uses reading skills and strategies to understand a variety of literary passages and texts (e.g., folktales, fiction, nonfiction, fables, biographies).
- Understands the basic concept of plot (e.g., main problem, conflict, resolution, cause-and-effect).
- Makes connections between characters or simple events in a literary work and people or events in his or her own life.

Uses reading skills and strategies to understand and interpret a variety of informational texts.

- Uses reading skills and strategies to understand a variety of informational texts (e.g., textbooks, biographical sketches, directions, procedures).
- Uses text organizers (e.g., headings, topic and summary sentences, graphic features, typeface, chapter titles) to determine the main ideas and to locate information in a text.
- Summarizes and paraphrases information in texts (e.g., includes the main idea and significant supporting details of a reading selection).
- Uses prior knowledge and experience to understand and respond to new information.
- Understands structural patterns or organization in informational texts (e.g., chronological, logical, or sequential order; compare-and-contrast; cause-and-effect; proposition and support).

Source: *Content Knowledge: A Compendium of Standards and Benchmarks for K–12 Education*, 4th Edition (Mid-continent Research for Education and Learning, 2006).

How to Use This Book

Getting Started

Choose a passage by identifying a theme that you would like to focus on and selecting the specific skill or skills you would like students to practice (see skills matrix on page 16). Make single-sided copies of the passage and activity sheet so that students can easily refer to the passage as they answer the questions.

Introducing the Skills

Once you have identified the skill you would like to address, plan a mini-lesson to introduce it. In the lesson, define the skill and give examples. Then model the way a proficient reader might think about that skill, and provide opportunities for students to practice. If possible, choose your examples from texts that students are reading as a class. (See pages 10–15 for examples of mini-lessons for each of the targeted skills.) As you wrap up your mini-lesson, explain to students that they will have a chance to use this skill and others as they answer the questions on the activity sheet.

Using the Activities

Begin each reading activity by discussing the Before You Read prompt at the top of each passage page. These prompts are designed to engage students in the topic and activate prior knowledge. This is an important step since studies indicate that many students need prompting to connect prior knowledge to the text at hand (Pressley, 2000). Think of this step as establishing a stage on which students can build new knowledge. Read the question aloud and lead a brief discussion, encouraging all students to participate. One way to engage everyone is to have students share their response with another student.

As you turn your attention to the passage, choose a reading style that will work best for your class. You may choose to have students read independently or take turns reading aloud.

After reading, have students answer the questions either independently or in small groups. Encourage students to underline the place in the passage where they found support for each answer.

Finally, have students check their work. If students have been working independently so far, consider having them form small groups for this stage. That way students can discuss the answers and explain their strategies and reasoning for answering the questions the way they did. Invite each small group to discuss and explain one of the questions to the rest of the class.

Extending the Activity

Writing about what they have read is one of the best ways for students to check comprehension and develop connections between the text and their own lives. Each activity in the book includes a writing prompt that encourages students to think about how the material applies to their own experiences. You can also extend the activity by having students ask their own questions about the text (kids love assuming the role of teacher!) and discuss the answers in small groups or as a class.

Applying the Skills

Use these passages for scaffolded instruction to give students practice with the skills before they use them independently in their own reading. Continue to teach strategic reading even after you have addressed all the skills. As you read texts aloud as a class, continue to think aloud to show students your reading strategies. Ask students to pause between paragraphs or sections, and step in to model how you predict, compare and contrast, infer, and so on. Encourage students to try this in class discussion and then as they read independently.

Consider having students keep journals in which they can respond to their independent reading (have them leave margins or space at the bottom of the page for your questions, observations, and encouraging words). Periodically hold individual conferences with students to discuss the book and the students' responses. From these observations, determine which skills students need more instruction in and practice with.

Additional Reading Strategies

Several effective strategies for improving comprehension have already been mentioned. These include having readers work cooperatively on the same reading task, participate in discussion, and answer questions about the text. Other strategies that may help boost comprehension include the following:

1. **Monitoring understanding:** Studies show that good readers ask, "Does this make sense to me?" as they read (National Reading Panel, 2000). If the answer is no, these readers pursue other strategies such as rereading sections of the text or adjusting the rate at which they are reading. One way to encourage students to monitor understanding is to use reading response journals (see page 8 for journal ideas).

2. **Using graphic organizers:** Charts, main idea webs, Venn diagrams, and other visual representations help readers see relationships among various elements of the text (National Reading Panel, 2000).

3. **Teaching story structure:** Studies prove that students who know the elements of fiction (such as setting, characters, problem, solution, and resolution) and nonfiction (main ideas, supporting details, headings, captions, and so on) have improved comprehension (National Reading Panel, 2000). An analogy to demonstrate the benefit of this strategy is this: Imagine that you are entering an unfamiliar kitchen. Even though you have never set foot in it before, you have a general idea of what it probably contains and where you might locate various elements (dishes in cabinets, food in the refrigerator, trash can under the sink) because you have been in many other kitchens. For good readers, encountering a new fiction or nonfiction text is a similar experience.

4. **Asking questions:** Good readers don't just answer questions given to them by tests or teachers; they also ask and answer their own questions as they read (National Reading Panel, 2000).

5. **Summarizing:** When students summarize a text, they focus on important ideas and filter out irrelevant information (National Reading Panel, 2000).

6. **Previewing and predicting:** Readers often find it useful to check out a text's title, subtitles, and illustrations before they begin to read, in order to get an idea of what to expect. As they read, they may ask themselves, "What do I think will happen next?"

7. **Skimming and scanning:** Readers skim a book or article to establish a purpose for reading and get their bearings. They can also scan before or after reading. Scanning entails looking quickly for specific information.

MINI-LESSON

Identifying Main Idea and Details

Introduce the Skill

Grab students' attention by displaying two open umbrellas in the front of the classroom. Label each umbrella with one of these two main idea sentences. (Write each sentence on a slip of paper and tape it on.)

I love winter sports.
The ancient Mayans enjoyed chocolate.

Then distribute the following sentences on paper strips to student volunteers. Invite students to read aloud the sentence they have been given and then sit under the appropriate umbrella.

My cousin and I belong to the ski club.
I go ice-skating every time I visit my grandma.
I just learned how to snowboard!
They found cacao beans in the rain forest.
They roasted and ground the beans.
They added water and cornmeal to make a chocolate drink.

Ask students to explain how they decided where each sentence belonged and to describe the difference between the umbrella sentences and the sentences held by the volunteers. Point out that the umbrellas represent main ideas and the sentence strips represent supporting details.

Think Aloud

Model how students can think about main ideas and details. Say, "To find the main idea of a book or passage, I ask myself, 'What is this text mostly about?' For example, these three sentences are all about winter sports. That's why we put them under this main idea umbrella. And these three sentences all give facts about how the Mayans used chocolate, so we put them under this main idea umbrella."

Spotlight the Skill

- The main idea is often—but not always—the first sentence in a paragraph. It can also appear at the end or even in the middle of the paragraph. Sometimes the main idea is not stated outright at all but is implicit in the text; in order to identify that type of main idea, the reader has to determine what all the details in a paragraph have in common.
- Distinguishing between main idea and details helps the reader understand and remember the most important points in a book or passage.
- Titles, chapter titles, and subtitles often serve as clues to a text's main idea.
- Tests have different ways to ask for main ideas and details. Main idea questions include:
    - What is another good title for this passage?
    - What is the main idea?
    - What is this passage mostly about?

  Detail questions usually ask about the 5 *W*'s (*who, what, where, when,* and *why*) as well as *how*.
- To visualize the relationship between main ideas and details, create a web with the main idea in the center and the supporting details branching out from it.

Use the Skills Matrix

The passages and activities starting on page 18 provide opportunities for practice with this and other reading comprehension skills. Check the matrix on page 16 to find out which skill is covered by each question in the activities. For example, questions 1, 4, and 7 on page 19 give students practice in identifying main idea and details.

MINI-LESSON

Predicting

Introduce the Skill

Display some fiction and nonfiction book covers, or write book titles on the board, such as *Making the Team* and *Creatures of the Sea*. Ask students to make predictions about each book based on the title. Ask: "What do you think the book will be about? Do you think it will be fiction (a story) or nonfiction (informative)? Why?" If you are using book covers, have students look at the cover illustrations or photos. Ask: "Does the art help you make predictions about the text?" Point out that most readers make predictions about a text when they read the title or look at the cover. They also continue to make predictions as they read.

Think Aloud

Model how students can think about predicting when they read. Say, "When I read the title *Making the Team*, it makes me think of competitive sports, so I think the book will be a story about a kid who is competing to get on a sports team. When I read the title *Creatures of the Sea*, I predict that it will be a book of facts about animals that live in the sea."

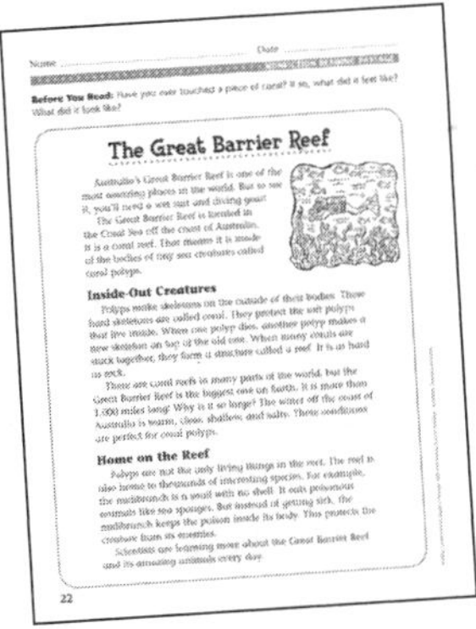

The Great Barrier Reef

Inside-Out Creatures

Home on the Reef

22

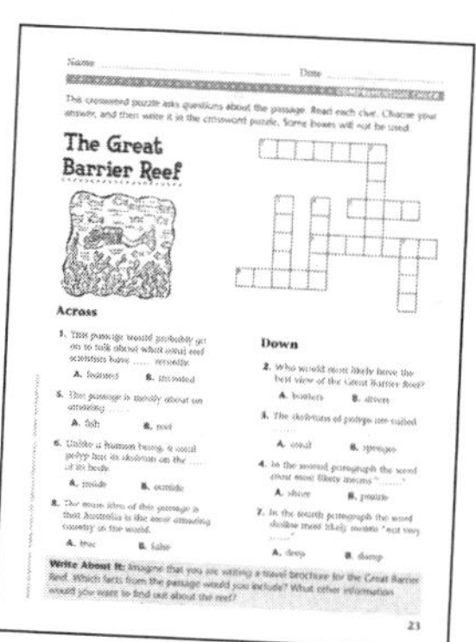

The Great Barrier Reef

Across

Down

23

Spotlight the Skill

- Predicting is a strategy that students can use both before and while reading text. Making predictions builds interest and encourages students to become deeply involved in the text, as they learn to use clues in the text as support for their predictions and, later, compare their predictions with what actually happens. These habits boost comprehension.
- Point out that readers can use titles, subtitles, illustrations, and text, as well as their own prior knowledge, to make predictions. When making predictions before reading, students rely on titles, illustrations, and prior knowledge. During reading, students use the text to support or adjust their initial predictions and to make new ones.
- Encourage students to make predictions in their reading response journals. In later entries, have them comment on whether or not their predictions came true. Students can also make a mental note of their predictions or discuss them in groups.

Use the Skills Matrix

The passages and activities starting on page 18 provide opportunities for practice with this and other reading comprehension skills. Check the matrix on page 16 to find out which skill is covered by each question in the activities. For example, question 1 on page 23 gives students practice in predicting.

MINI-LESSON

Making Inferences

Introduce the Skill

Start your exploration with an exercise or two designed to get students thinking "between the lines." Try one of these, or make up your own:

Read aloud:

> *When Dominique finally spotted her mom, her heart stopped pounding and her breathing slowly returned to normal. She thanked the saleswoman for her help and ran to her mom.*

Ask:
- Where are Dominique and her mom? How do you know?
- What do you think has just happened? Why do you think so?
- How does Dominique feel right now? What clues helped you decide?

Read aloud:

> *Henry stared at the pile of books in front of him and fought the urge to go into the kitchen for a snack. If he didn't start now, he would never finish in time to watch the big game.*

Ask:
- Where do you think Henry is? Why?
- What is Henry doing? How do you know?

Think Aloud

Model how students can make inferences when they read. For example, if you are using the first example above, you might say, "There is a salesperson, so I think that Dominique and her mom are probably in a store. It sounds to me as if Dominique was lost, because it says she 'finally spotted her mom.' I know that when I am scared, my heart pounds and I start breathing really fast, so Dominique was probably scared when she was lost. Now it sounds as though she feels relieved."

Spotlight the Skill

- Point out to students that making inferences, or "reading between the lines," can help them make sense of what they read. They can use clues from a story—along with what they may already know—to figure out something that is not directly stated in the text. Readers often do this without thinking about it.
- As students read a passage, stop periodically to make some inferences together. Ask, for example: "How do you think that character felt after that experience?" or "Why do you think the writer included that particular fact?"
- Explain to students that they may find it helpful to underline clues in the story that led them to make a particular inference.
- Sometimes readers make an inference that is incorrect. Clues provided later in the passage or book may help them realize their mistake and adjust their comprehension. For example, in the second example at left, most readers would infer that Henry is tackling his homework. It is a fair inference to make given the clues available. If, however, the next paragraph revealed that the books were Henry's dad's old yearbooks, good readers would reconsider the inference.

Use the Skills Matrix

The passages and activities starting on page 18 provide opportunities for practice with this and other reading comprehension skills. Check the matrix on page 16 to find out which skill is covered by each question in the activities. For example, questions 2 and 8 on page 29 give students practice in making inferences.

MINI-LESSON

Comparing and Contrasting

Introduce the Skill

Group students in pairs and challenge each pair of students to come up with at least one way they are alike and one way they are different. Responses may revolve around interests, talents, physical traits, pets, birthdays, and so on. If you have an aide or other adult in the classroom (or an extra student) to work with, sit with him or her and do the same activity. Afterward, invite each pair to share their findings with the class. Point out that readers are always thinking about the ways characters, places, and things in the texts they read are alike and different.

Think Aloud

Model how students can compare and contrast when they read. Say, for example, "When I compare Matt and Dennis, I see that they both have older sisters and like to play basketball. When I contrast them, I see that Matt has black hair and Dennis has red hair."

The Sleepover

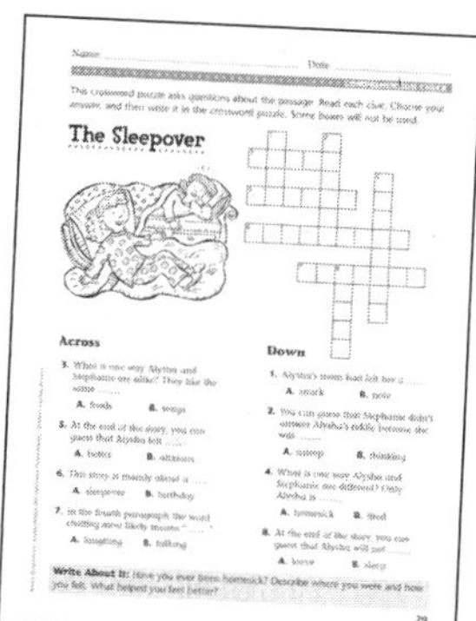

The Sleepover

Spotlight the Skill

- Explore the difference between comparing and contrasting. When we compare two or more things, we think about the ways they are alike or similar. When we contrast two or more things, we focus on the ways they are different. Good readers perform both strategies as they read. They compare and contrast the people, places, and things they read about to one another, as well as to the people, places, and things they already knew about from other books, from movies and television, and from real life ("prior knowledge").
- Proficient readers are alert to certain signal words that suggest that the writer is comparing or contrasting people or things. Look for the words *like, unlike, both, all,* and *neither,* as well as comparative and superlative adjectives and adverbs such as *faster, nearest,* and *more gently*.
- To help students visualize the similarities and differences between people, places, or things in a text, have them create Venn diagrams.

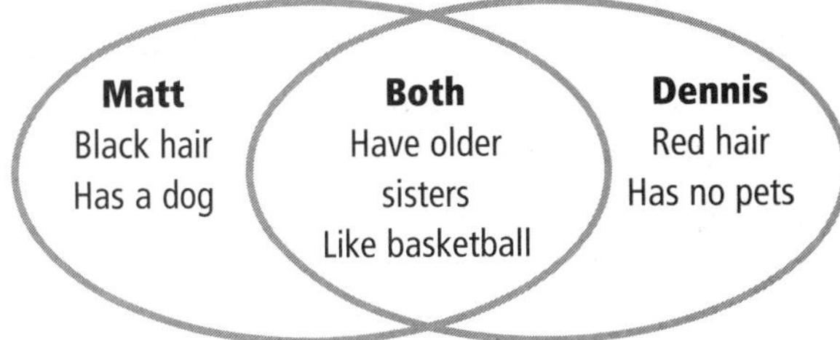

Use the Skills Matrix

The passages and activities starting on page 18 provide opportunities for practice with this and other reading comprehension skills. Check the matrix on page 16 to find out which skill is covered by each question in the activities. For example, questions 3 and 4 on page 29 give students practice in comparing and contrasting.

MINI-LESSON

Identifying Fact and Opinion

Introduce the Skill

Begin the lesson by explaining to students that you are going to tell them about a dog that lives on your block. Ask them to listen carefully to the statements you make about the dog. State several facts and at least one opinion without naming them as such.

Duffy weighs 25 pounds.
Duffy is a beagle.
Duffy is the cutest dog on the block.
Duffy has big brown eyes.
Everyone should get a dog like Duffy.

Follow up by asking students to share what they noticed about your statements. Were the statements similar or different in any way? How? Explain that the class will be exploring these two types of statements, called facts and opinions.

Think Aloud

Model how students can think about facts and opinions when they read. Say, "When I read a statement in a book or passage, I am sometimes not sure whether it is a fact or an opinion. To decide, I ask myself whether the statement could be proved true. If so, then it is a fact. I can prove that Duffy weighs 25 pounds by weighing him or checking his vet records. I can also prove that he is a beagle and has brown eyes by observing him. But I can't really prove that he's the cutest dog on the block, or that everyone should get a dog like him. Plenty of people might disagree. That makes those two statements examples of opinions."

Spotlight the Skill

- Discuss why it is important to recognize facts and opinions. Ask: "What might happen if we believed everything we read as fact?"
- Brainstorm different ways that a fact could be proved true. For example, we can measure people and things, interview experts, and check record books. Make sure that students understand that you do not expect them to prove the facts that they read; the important skill is the ability to distinguish things that could be proved true from things that are not provable.
- One way to recognize statements of opinion is to be on the lookout for judgmental words like *should* or *should not*, abstract adjectives like *beautiful* or *nice*, and comparative and superlative adjectives such as *better, worse, most,* and *least*. When exploring opinions with students, point out that it is helpful to ask, "Who holds this opinion?" as they read. It may be a character in a story or a newsmaker quoted in an article. Recognizing the source of the opinion—and realizing that they may choose to agree or disagree—can help students become more critical and comprehending readers.
- Newspapers are a great place to explore facts and opinions. Have students look for facts in news stories and opinions in editorials, ads, and direct quotations. Challenge them to highlight the two types of statements in different colors.

Use the Skills Matrix

The passages and activities starting on page 18 provide opportunities for practice with this and other reading comprehension skills. Check the matrix on page 16 to find out which skill is covered by each question in the activities. For example, question 8 on page 19 gives students practice in identifying fact and opinion.

MINI-LESSON

Using Context Clues

Introduce the Skill

Write the words *blunder, sulk,* and *dysentery* on the board, and ask students if anyone can define the words. Invite students to try to guess their meanings through context. Read aloud a sentence for each word, and have students offer possible definitions.

> *Ian made a* ***blunder*** *when he mentioned the surprise party to the birthday girl.*
>
> *When Rachel did not get her way, she stormed off to her room to* ***sulk****.*
>
> *The ship doctor was called because many passengers were suffering from* ***dysentery****.*

Reveal the definitions of the words. Discuss why it was easier to understand the meaning of each new word in the context of a sentence.

Think Aloud

Model how students can think about context clues when they read. Say, "When I don't know the meaning of a word in a story, I look at the words and sentences around it for clues. Mentioning a surprise party to the birthday girl is not a good idea, so I am going to guess that a *blunder* is a mistake. It sounds as if Rachel is mad, so I can guess that *sulking* is like being in a bad mood. And if a doctor was called, I can guess that *dysentery* is some kind of illness."

Spotlight the Skill

- Explain that the words and sentences surrounding the mystery word that help the reader determine the word's meaning are called context clues. Context is the setting, or situation, in which the word is found. It includes the sentence, paragraph, and the whole passage or book.
- Sometimes words are clearly defined within the sentence or paragraph. This type of context clue is easy to spot. For example, in this sentence, the word's definition is set off by commas:

  The judge spoke to the defendant, the person charged with the crime, on Tuesday morning.

  In this example, the word's meaning is stated in the next sentence:

  Katie is learning calligraphy. It is a fancy form of handwriting.
- In other cases, readers need to use other details from the sentence and paragraph to guess the word's meaning. In this example, the words *feet* and *rain* help the reader guess that galoshes are rain boots:

  Ian pulled galoshes on his feet before heading out into the rain.
- Once readers think they have identified the meaning of a word, they can use the "replace and check" technique to see if the meaning makes sense. Simply replace the mystery word with the proposed synonym to see if the sentence makes sense.

Use the Skills Matrix

The passages and activities starting on page 18 provide opportunities for practice with this and other reading comprehension skills. Check the matrix on page 16 to find out which skill is covered by each question in the activities. For example, questions 1 and 8 on page 21 give students practice in using context clues.

Skills Matrix

Use the matrix below to find out which skill is covered by each question in the activities. Question numbers are provided in each skill column.

	Main Idea and Details	Predicting	Making Inferences	Comparing and Contrasting	Identifying Fact and Opinion	Using Context Clues
Crossword Puzzles	Question Numbers					
Feeling Hot, Hot, Hot (Nonfiction—page 19)	1,4,7	5	6	2	8	3
Teddy's Story (Nonfiction—page 21)	2,4,7		5	3	6	1,8
The Great Barrier Reef (Nonfiction—page 23)	3,5,8	1	2	6		4,7
A Day at the Zoo (Fiction—page 25)	5,7,8		4	1	3	2,6
A Cool Hotel! (Nonfiction—page 27)	1,2,5,7		4		6	3
The Sleepover (Fiction—page 29)	1,6	5	2,8	3,4		7
Word Searches						
The Sinking City (Nonfiction—page 31)	1,2	7	5	6	4	3,8
Horrible Hiccups (Fiction—page 33)	1,5,6		2	3	4	7
Why Leaves Change Color (Nonfiction—page 35)	1,2,6	7	8	3	4	5
Paul Bunyan (Fiction—page 37)	1,2,6		7	4		3,5
Lily on the Loose (Fiction—page 39)	1,2,4	7	5		8	3,6
Trunk Talk (Nonfiction—page 41)	2,5,6,7	8	3,4	3		1
Comprehension Mazes						
Vitamin ABCs (Nonfiction—page 43)	1,2		6	3	5	4
Happy New Year! (Fiction—page 45)	1,6	5	2	3		4
Animal Pals (Nonfiction—page 47)	1,6		3	5		2,4
Trash Trouble (Fiction—page 49)	1,2		4		5	3,6
The First Olympics (Nonfiction—page 51)	1,2		6	4		3,5
Forest Frogs Stay Safe (Nonfiction—page 53)	1,2			5,6		3,4
Riddle Quizzes						
A School at the Zoo (Nonfiction—page 55)	1,2,4			7	5	3,6
100th Day Disaster (Fiction—page 57)	2	6	1,3	5		4,7
April Fools' Day (Nonfiction—page 59)	2,3		5		4	1,6
The Ant and the Dove (Fiction—page 61)	1,2,4,5	7	8			3,6
A Dino Discovery (Nonfiction—page 63)	1,2,8		4,7	5	3	6
We All Win! (Fiction—page 65)	1	6		2,3	7	4,5
Tic-Tac-Toe Games						
They Have the Beat! (Nonfiction—page 67)	1,4,8		3,6,9	2	5	7
The Friendship Box (Fiction—page 69)	1,4,6,8	9	2	5		3,7
Garbage in the Garden (Nonfiction—page 71)	1,2,4,9	8	6	3	7	5
Too Much TV (Fiction—page 73)	1,3,6	7	4,5		8	2,9
Finding Freddy (Fiction—page 75)	1,5,7	9	3,8		4	2,6
A Cool Inventor (Nonfiction—page 77)	1,2,3,7,8		5,9			4,6

References and Additional Resources

Works Cited

Harris, T. L. & Hodges, R. E. (1995). *The literacy dictionary.* Newark, DE. International Reading Association.

National Reading Panel. 2000. *Teaching children to read: An evidence-based assessment of the scientific research literature on reading and its implications for reading instruction.* Washington, D.C.: National Institute of Child Health and Human Development. (Also available online at www.nationalreadingpanel.org.)

Pressley, M. 2000. *Comprehension instruction: What makes sense now, what might make sense soon.* In *Handbook of reading research,* M. L. Kamil et al., eds., vol. 3, chap. 30. Mahwah, NJ: Erlbaum.

RAND Reading Study Group. 2002. *Reading for understanding: Toward an R and D program in reading comprehension.* Santa Monica, CA: RAND Corporation.

Teacher Resources

Beech, Linda Ward. *Reading Passages That Build Comprehension.* New York: Scholastic, 2005. This series includes volumes on main idea and details, predicting, inference, context clues, compare and contrast, and fact and opinion.

Outsen, Nicole and Stephanie Yulga. *Teaching Comprehension Strategies All Readers Need.* New York: Scholastic, 2002.

Name ______________________ Date ______________

NONFICTION READING PASSAGE

Before You Read: How do you feel when you have a fever? What do you think is happening inside your body?

Feeling Hot, Hot, Hot

If you have ever had the flu, you know that a fever can make you feel awful. Your whole body aches, and you might shiver with chills. You probably feel like staying in bed. But did you know that the fever is actually helping you get better? It is one way your body fights off germs.

Germs Attack

As germs travel through your body, they can make you ill in many ways. For example, tiny bacteria might attack your inner ear, giving you an infection.

But don't worry. Your body fights back! First, the white cells in your blood send a message to your brain. They tell your brain that germs have invaded. In response, your brain gives off chemicals that make you feel cold. To warm up, your body burns fat, stops sweating, and starts shaking or shivering. That makes your temperature higher than normal. A normal human temperature is about 98.6 degrees Fahrenheit. A sick person might have a temperature of 101 degrees or even higher.

Zapping Germs

The extra heat helps to "fry" the germs and get rid of them. But sometimes your body can't fight the germs on its own. You may need to see a doctor. He or she can give you medicine called an antibiotic to kill the germs. You might think the antibiotic tastes terrible, but it will help you get better.

Once your brain gets the message that the germs are gone, you begin sweating. That brings your temperature back to normal.

Name ______________________ Date ______________

COMPREHENSION CHECK

This crossword puzzle asks questions about the passage. Read each clue. Choose your answer, and then write it in the crossword puzzle.

Feeling Hot, Hot, Hot

Across

4. Germs can cause an ear ____.

A. drum **B.** infection

6. Most likely, ears are *not* the only body parts that can get infections.

A. true **B.** false

7. Another good title for this passage would be "All About ____."

A. Colds **B.** Fevers

8. How would you complete this sentence to state a *fact*? Antibiotics are ____.

A. medicine **B.** unpleasant

Down

1. The main idea of this passage is that fevers fight ____.

A. germs **B.** sweat

2. A temperature of 101 degrees Fahrenheit is ____ than a normal human temperature.

A. lower **B.** higher

3. In the first paragraph the word *aches* most likely means "____."

A. helps **B.** hurts

5. You can predict that once the fever has killed the germs, you will feel ____.

A. better **B.** worse

Write About It: Pretend you are a germ that has entered a person's body. Write a paragraph describing what you think and feel as the person's body fights back.

Name ________________________ Date ________________

Before You Read: Why do you think teddy bears are so popular? How do you think they got their name?

Teddy's Story

Teddy bears come in all sizes and colors. But they are all named for the same person—Theodore Roosevelt, our nation's 25th president.

President Theodore Roosevelt was often called by his nickname, Teddy. He was a hunter, but he liked animals a lot. In 1902 Roosevelt went hunting in Mississippi. Some of the president's aides went along to help him. A group of news reporters went, too. They wanted to write news reports about the president's trip.

No News

There was just one problem. After several days the president still had not killed any animals. The news reporters wrote stories telling the nation that Roosevelt was not a very skilled hunter. Then one day a bear cub wandered into the president's camping area. The president's aides told him to shoot the young bear. But Roosevelt refused.

A popular newspaper cartoonist named Clifford Berryman drew a funny picture to tell the story. Soon everyone was talking about Roosevelt's love for bears.

A Bear Is Born

A toy maker named Morris Michtom got an idea when he heard the story. He and his wife, Rose, made a stuffed toy bear. They named it "Teddy's bear" and sold it in their shop in Brooklyn, New York. Other customers wanted bears, too. So Michtom started the Ideal Toy Company and began making teddy bears. They were a huge hit. Now many companies make their own "teddy" bears.

Name ______________________ Date ______________

COMPREHENSION CHECK

This crossword puzzle asks questions about the passage. Read each clue. Choose your answer, and then write it in the crossword puzzle.

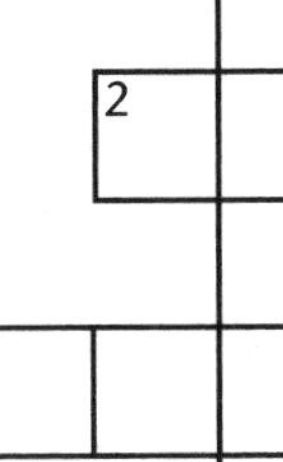

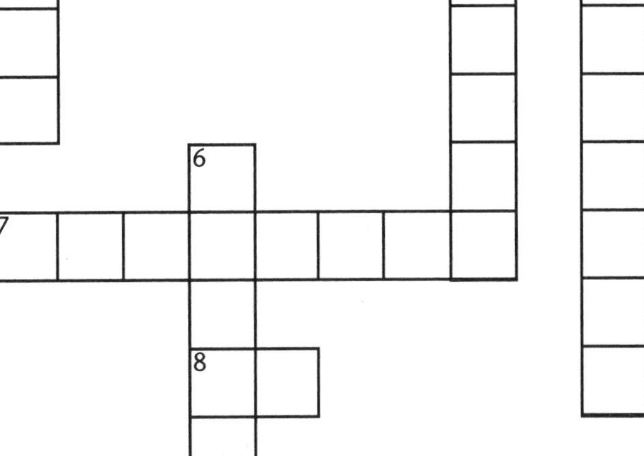

Across

2. President Roosevelt went camping in ____.

A. Montana **B.** Mississippi

5. You can tell from the story that President Roosevelt most likely bought toys.

A. true **B.** false

7. The first teddy bear was sold in ____, New York.

A. Ithaca **B.** Brooklyn

8. In the third paragraph the word *refused* most likely means "said ____."

A. maybe **B.** no

Down

1. In the second paragraph the word that most likely means "helpers" is ____.

A. *aides* **B.** *reporters*

3. Teddy bears may look different, but they are all named for the same ____.

A. city **B.** person

4. This passage explains how teddy bears were ____.

A. invented **B.** repaired

6. How would you complete this sentence to state a *fact*?
The bear that wandered into President Roosevelt's camp was ____.

A. young **B.** adorable

Write About It: What kind of toy would you want to have named after you? Why? Write a paragraph about your choice.

Name ______________________ Date ______________

Before You Read: Have you ever touched a piece of coral? If so, what did it feel like? What did it look like?

The Great Barrier Reef

Australia's Great Barrier Reef is one of the most amazing places in the world. But to see it, you'll need a wet suit and diving gear!

The Great Barrier Reef is located in the Coral Sea off the coast of Australia. It is a coral reef. That means it is made of the bodies of tiny sea creatures called coral polyps.

Inside-Out Creatures

Polyps make skeletons on the outside of their bodies. These hard skeletons are called coral. They protect the soft polyps that live inside. When one polyp dies, another polyp makes a new skeleton on top of the old one. When many corals are stuck together, they form a structure called a reef. It is as hard as rock.

There are coral reefs in many parts of the world, but the Great Barrier Reef is the biggest one on Earth. It is more than 1,000 miles long! Why is it so large? The water off the coast of Australia is warm, clear, shallow, and salty. These conditions are perfect for coral polyps.

Home on the Reef

Polyps are not the only living things in the reef. The reef is also home to thousands of interesting species. For example, the nudibranch is a snail with no shell. It eats poisonous animals like sea sponges. But instead of getting sick, the nudibranch keeps the poison inside its body. This protects the creature from its enemies.

Scientists are learning more about the Great Barrier Reef and its amazing animals every day.

Name ______________________ Date ______________

COMPREHENSION CHECK

This quiz asks questions about the passage. Circle your answer, and then circle the word in the word search puzzle. Words can appear across, down, or on a diagonal.

Paul Bunyan

1. The story of Paul Bunyan is an example of a ____ tale.

A. true **B.** tall

2. Paul Bunyan's mother used wagon wheels for his ____.

A. buttons **B.** plates

3. You can guess from the passage that a ____ is someone who cuts down trees.

A. lumberjack **B.** camp

4. How are Paul and Babe alike? They are both ____.

A. huge **B.** babies

5. In the fourth paragraph the word *devour* most likely means "to eat something ____."

A. slowly **B.** quickly

6. According to the tale, Paul's footprints turned into ____.

A. lakes **B.** bowls

7. You can guess a giant named Paul Bunyan really lived 150 years ago.

A. true **B.** false

Write About It: Write your own tall tale! Imagine that a new neighbor who has some unusual characteristics moves to town. Describe this person.

Name ______________________________ Date ______________

Before You Read: Do you have a pet at home or at school? If so, what responsibilities do you have for taking care of the pet?

Lily on the Loose

Min and her father carefully made their way across the school parking lot. In Mr. Kwon's arms was a clear plastic cage. A curious little hamster pressed its nose against the plastic. Min carried a bag full of hamster food and other supplies.

Min was excited. Mrs. Vuz had asked her to care for Lily, the class pet, for the weekend. It was an important job!

Following Directions

When they got home, Min took a yellow paper from her backpack. It was from Mrs. Vuz. It gave instructions for taking care of Lily. The paper said to feed Lily every day and to give her honey sticks as special treats. It also said to clean Lily's cage.

Min had fun caring for Lily. Time flew, and before long, it was Sunday afternoon. Min decided to clean Lily's cage. First, she took the lid off. Then, she put Lily in an empty tissue box while she cleaned out the cage.

"Time to go back in, Lily!" Min said when she finished wiping the

cage clean. But when she looked in the tissue box, she saw that Lily was gone!

Where's Lily?

Min looked under her bed. She looked behind her bookcase. No Lily. Min's parents joined the search. But they had no luck. Lily was missing!

The next morning Min was too sad to eat breakfast. When it was time to leave for school, Mr. Kwon brought Lily's empty cage out to the van. Min sighed and began to put on her shoes.

Just as Min went to slip her right foot into her sneaker, a tiny face peeked out. It was Lily!

"You silly hamster!" Min cried. "No more hide-and-seek!"

Name ______________________ Date ______________

COMPREHENSION CHECK

This quiz asks questions about the passage. Circle your answer, and then circle the word in the word search puzzle. Words can appear across, down, or on a diagonal.

Lily on the Loose

1. Another good title for this passage would be "Lily's Great ____."

A. Escape **B.** Summer

2. The passage is mainly about a girl and a ____.

A. fish **B.** hamster

3. In the third paragraph the word *instructions* most likely means "____."

A. directions **B.** supplies

4. For a special treat, Lily gets ____ sticks.

A. honey **B.** carrot

5. Mrs. Vuz is most likely Min's ____.

A. mother **B.** teacher

6. The passage says that "time flew" while Min cared for Lily. That means that time seemed to pass ____.

A. quickly **B.** slowly

7. What will probably happen next? Min will bring Lily to ____.

A. school **B.** practice

8. Complete this sentence to state a *fact*. In the story Lily was ____.

A. missing **B.** cute

Write About It: Imagine that Min had not found Lily. How would she feel? What could she say to her class to explain what had happened?

Name ______________________ Date ______________

NONFICTION READING PASSAGE

Before You Read: How do people communicate with one another? Do you think animals can communicate, too?

Trunk Talk

When people talk to one another, they share ideas and feelings. This is called communication. Scientists know that humans are not the only ones who can communicate. Many animals can, too. Birds chirp and sing to each other. Cats purr to show they are happy and puff out their fur to scare away enemies. Now experts are learning that elephants can also communicate.

Elephant Chatter

Elephants need to communicate with each other because they live in groups. A group can have up to ten female elephants and their young. The elephants in the group travel together to find food and water. The oldest female elephant is usually the group's leader. She does a lot of the "talking."

Of course, elephants do not use words, as humans do. But they do make sounds. They can make dozens of different types of calls, such as rumbles, grunts, and loud trumpets. For example, an elephant rumbles to say, "Let's go!" The others in the group rumble back to say, "We're coming." Some of the sounds that elephants make are very, very quiet. They are too soft for humans to hear.

Body Language

Elephants also use body language. For example, they twist their trunks together to say hello. They stick their ears straight out and shake their heads to scare off other animals. They smile to show that they are happy. And baby elephants touch their mothers' legs to ask for milk.

Scientists hope that one day they will learn a lot more about how elephants communicate. The next time you see an elephant at the zoo, say hello. See if the elephant answers back!

Name ______________________________ Date ________________

COMPREHENSION CHECK

This quiz asks questions about the passage. Circle your answer, and then circle the word in the word search puzzle. Words can appear across, down, or on a diagonal.

Trunk Talk

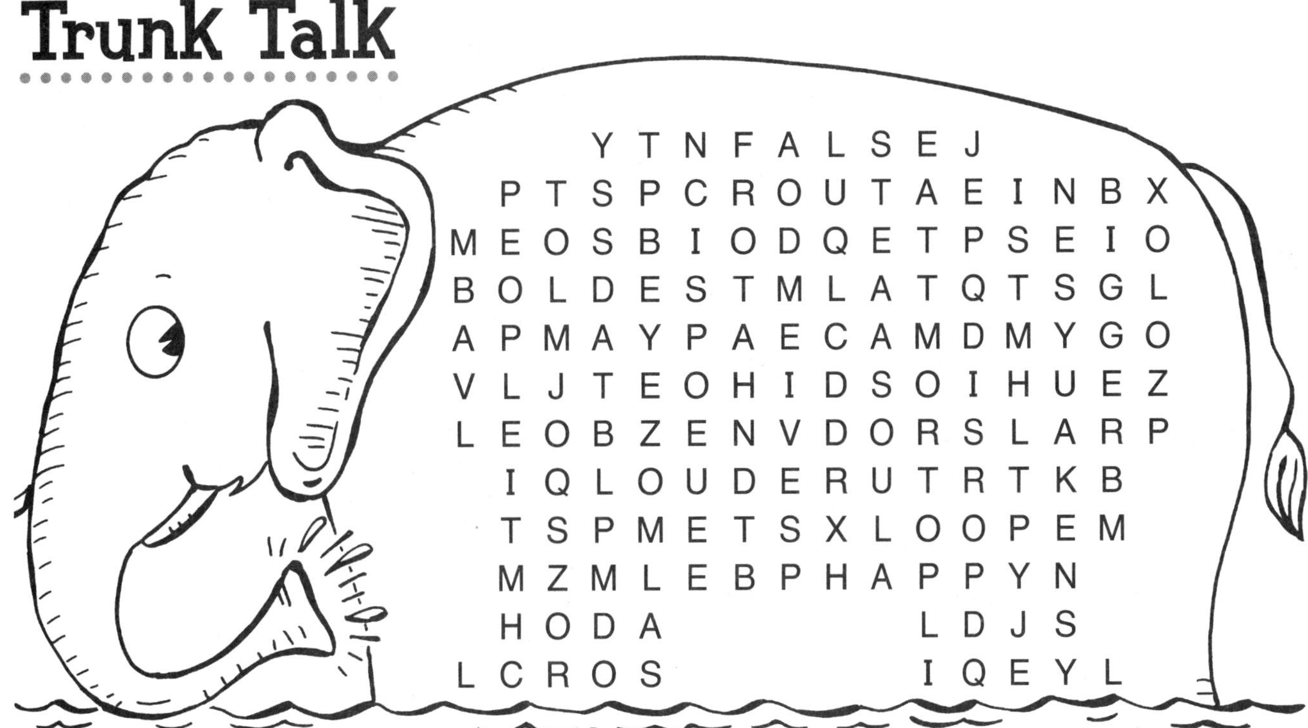

1. In the first paragraph the word *humans* means "____."

A. species **B.** people

2. This passage is mainly about how elephants ____.

A. travel **B.** communicate

3. You can guess from the passage that an elephant's trumpet is ____ than its rumble.

A. louder **B.** softer

4. You can guess from the story that cats probably puff out their fur in order to look ____.

A. nicer **B.** bigger

5. Cats purr to show that they are ____.

A. happy **B.** scared

6. The ____ female elephant in a group is usually the leader.

A. largest **B.** oldest

7. Baby elephants touch their mothers' legs to ask for ____.

A. water **B.** milk

8. Now that scientists can identify trumpets and rumbles, you can guess that they will probably stop studying elephants.

A. true **B.** false

Write About It: People use body language, too. List three other ways you can say something without using words.

Building Comprehension: Reading Passages With High-Interest Practice Activities Scholastic Teaching Resources

Name ______________________________ Date ____________________

NONFICTION READING PASSAGE

Before You Read: Why are vitamins good for you? What foods do you think have the most vitamins?

Vitamin ABCs

You've probably heard that broccoli is good for you because it's full of vitamins. Your breakfast cereal might claim to be packed with vitamins, too. But what exactly are vitamins? And why are they important?

Vitamins are substances found in foods. They help your body in hundreds of ways. For example, vitamins help give you strong bones, good eyesight, and the energy to kick your way through soccer practice.

Most vitamins have long names, so people usually shorten them by calling them by letters. Here's a look at some important vitamins.

From A to E

Vitamin A helps you see well and makes your skin healthy. You can get plenty of vitamin A from eating melons, carrots, spinach, and nuts.

There are eight different B vitamins. They work together to keep your blood healthy and give you energy. B vitamins are found in fish, beef, chicken, and pork. Whole wheat bread, cereals, and green veggies also have B vitamins.

Vitamin C is a germ fighter! It helps your body fight off illnesses and heal cuts. Oranges, strawberries, watermelon, and green peppers all have loads of vitamin C.

Vitamin D helps your bones and teeth grow strong. It is in milk, eggs, and salmon.

Vitamin E keeps your eyes, skin, and heart healthy. You get it when you eat nuts, bananas, and leafy green vegetables like spinach.

Getting Enough

It's important to eat a balanced diet so that you get all the vitamins you need. Some people also take a vitamin supplement. Your family and doctor can help you decide if you need one.

Building Comprehension: Reading Passages With High-Interest Practice Activities Scholastic Teaching Resources

Name ____________________ Date ____________

COMPREHENSION CHECK

Use what you learned in the story to make your way through the maze. Answer each question to choose your path. If you answer each one correctly, you will reach the healthy feast!

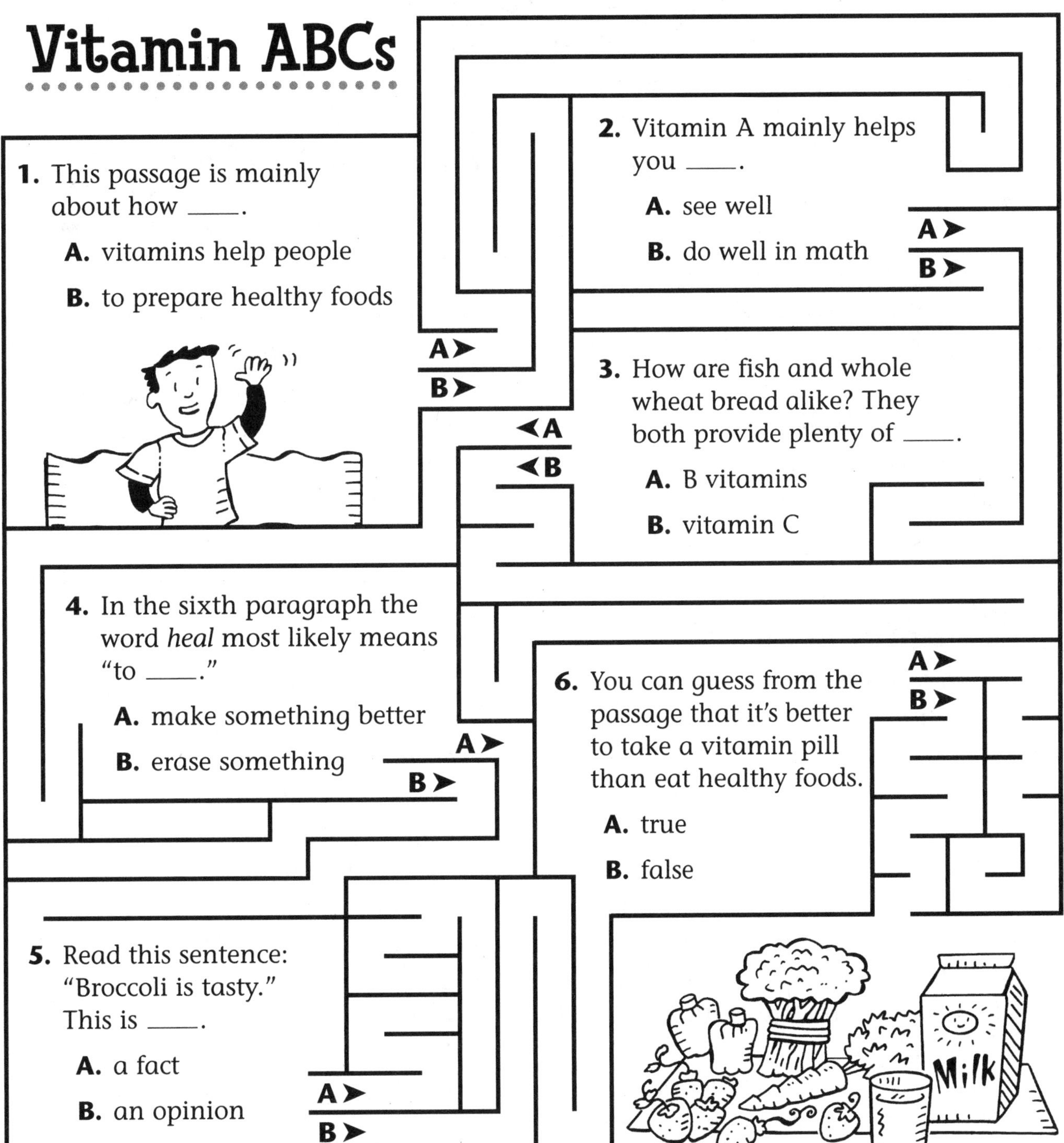

Vitamin ABCs
1. This passage is mainly about how ____.
A. vitamins help people
B. to prepare healthy foods
A➤
B➤
2. Vitamin A mainly helps you ____.
A. see well
B. do well in math
A➤
B➤
3. How are fish and whole wheat bread alike? They both provide plenty of ____.
A. B vitamins
B. vitamin C
◀A
◀B
4. In the sixth paragraph the word *heal* most likely means "to ____."
A. make something better
B. erase something
A➤
B➤
5. Read this sentence: "Broccoli is tasty." This is ____.
A. a fact
B. an opinion
A➤
B➤
6. You can guess from the passage that it's better to take a vitamin pill than eat healthy foods.
A. true
B. false
A➤
B➤
Milk

Write About It: Use the information from the story to plan a lunch that includes foods with vitamins A, B, C, D, and E.

Name ______________________________ Date ____________________

FICTION READING PASSAGE

Before You Read: How does your family celebrate the new year?

Happy New Year!

Jason was in line for lunch when his friend Steve walked up.

"Can you celebrate the new year with my family on Saturday?" Steve asked.

"Aren't you a little late?" said Jason. "New Year's Day was last month!"

"We commemorate the Chinese New Year as well," Steve explained. "It is on a different date every year."

"Sure! That sounds like fun," Jason said.

A Yummy Visit

On Saturday Jason's mom drove him to the Wongs' house. Mr. Wong answered the door.

"Gung Hay Fat Choy!" Mr. Wong said with a smile. "That means 'Happy New Year!'"

In the Wongs' living room, Jason saw a round tray of candies, nuts, and fruits. Steve explained that each item on the tray was supposed to bring luck.

First, Jason ate some peanuts. "In the Chinese tradition, peanuts are supposed to bring you a long life," Steve told him.

Next, Jason tried a fruit that

looked like a piece of dried orange. "That's a kumquat," Steve said. "Eating kumquats is supposed to bring you great fortune."

Parade Time

Later the Wongs took Jason and Steve to see the Chinese New Year parade. Jason watched dancers holding paper lion heads. He listened to the loud drums. But his favorite part came at the end, when a giant dragon rounded the corner! Mrs. Wong explained that 100 men and women were inside the fancy costume.

Before Jason went home, Mrs. Wong handed both boys shiny red envelopes. Inside each one was a crisp dollar bill.

"The envelopes are called *lai-see*," Steve explained. "Adults give them to kids to wish them a lucky new year."

"Thanks!" said Jason. "Mine is already off to a great start!"

Name ________________________ Date ______________

COMPREHENSION CHECK

Use what you learned in the story to make your way through the maze. Answer each question to choose your path. If you answer each one correctly, you will reach the dancing dragon!

Happy New Year!

1. "Gung Hay Fat Choy" is a way of saying ____.

A. "Happy New Year"

B. "Thank you"

A ➤

B ➤

2. You can guess that Jason's family celebrates New Year's Day on January 1.

A. true

B. false

A ➤

B ➤

3. According to Chinese tradition, how are peanuts and kumquats alike? They are both ____.

A. types of nuts

B. lucky foods

◄A

◄B

4. In the fourth paragraph the word *commemorate* most likely means "____."

A. to celebrate

B. to wish

A ➤

B ➤

5. What will probably happen next? Jason will ____.

A. go home

B. stay at the Wongs' house

A ➤

B ➤

6. Another good title for this passage would be ____.

A. "Best Friends"

B. "A Special Celebration"

A ➤

B ➤

Write About It: How does the Wongs' celebration compare with your celebration of the new year? Write a paragraph telling how they are alike and different.

Name ______________________ Date ______________

NONFICTION READING PASSAGE

Before You Read: Do you think animals help one another? If so, how?

Animal Pals

Imagine having a best friend who is hundreds of times bigger than you! It can happen in the animal world. Just look at the giant rhinoceros and its itty-bitty buddy, the oxpecker bird.

Big and Little

The rhinoceros is one of the biggest animals on Earth. The largest rhinos can weigh up to 5,000 pounds and reach the height of a human adult. When you see a rhino in the wild, it almost always has a small bird perched on its back. This bird is called an oxpecker. It is about nine inches long and has a yellow or red beak.

The rhino and the oxpecker make a great team. The oxpecker uses its sharp claws to grab onto the rhino's thick skin. It rides on the rhino's back all day long. The rhino does not seem to mind. Together, the two animals roam the grasslands and forests of Africa.

Working Together

The rhino helps the oxpecker by giving the bird a free ride—and a free meal. Whenever the oxpecker gets hungry, it can use its beak to pull ticks, flies, and other bugs off the rhino's back.

In return, the oxpecker keeps the rhino's back free of bugs. That is a big help because some bugs can give the rhino diseases. The oxpecker also protects the rhino from dangers. When the oxpecker spots a lion or other threat, it will squawk and fly into the air. This tells the rhino to watch out!

Scientists have a fancy word for the relationship between two different species that live together and help one another. It is symbiosis (SIM-bee-OH-sis). But you can just call it cooperation!

Name ______________________ Date ______________

COMPREHENSION CHECK

Use what you learned in the story to make your way through the maze. Answer each question to choose your path. If you answer each one correctly, you will reach your rhino friends in the tall grass!

Animal Pals

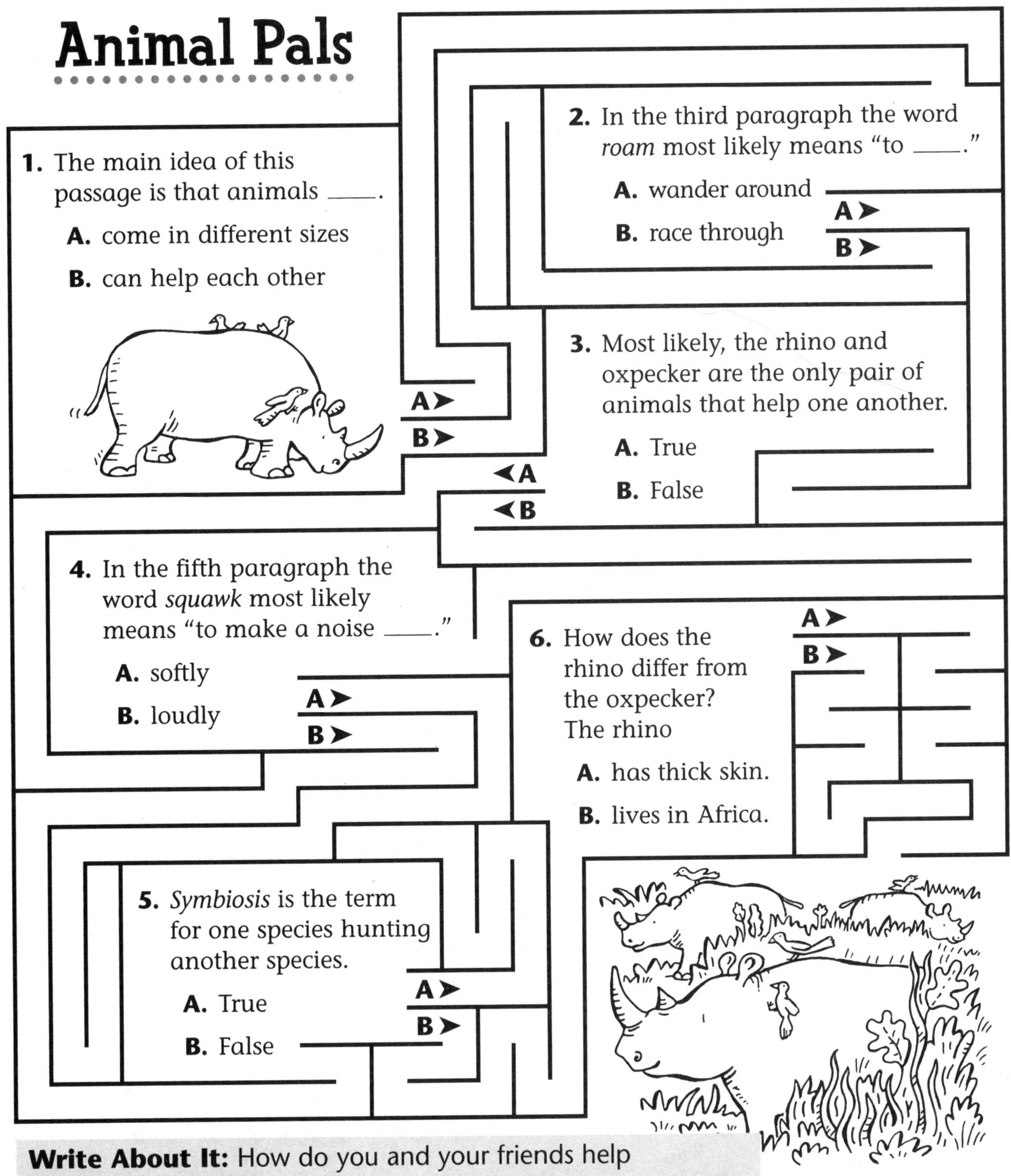

1. The main idea of this passage is that animals ____.
A. come in different sizes
B. can help each other
A➤
B➤
2. In the third paragraph the word *roam* most likely means "to ____."
A. wander around
B. race through
A➤
B➤
3. Most likely, the rhino and oxpecker are the only pair of animals that help one another.
A. True
B. False
◄A
◄B
4. In the fifth paragraph the word *squawk* most likely means "to make a noise ____."
A. softly
B. loudly
A➤
B➤
6. How does the rhino differ from the oxpecker? The rhino
A. has thick skin.
B. lives in Africa.
A➤
B➤
5. *Symbiosis* is the term for one species hunting another species.
A. True
B. False
A➤
B➤

Write About It: How do you and your friends help one another? Describe three ways on a separate sheet of paper.

Name ______________________ Date ______________

Before You Read: What do you think happens to trash if it's not thrown away properly? What problems could it cause?

Trash Trouble

One beautiful spring day Alexis was fishing with her dad. They had already caught four fish when they stopped for a lunch break.

Alexis put her sandwich wrapper in her brown bag. Then she headed for the trash can.

The Problem With Plastic

As Alexis walked, she noticed litter on the beach. There were candy wrappers, bottle caps, and soda cans. Then Alexis noticed something else. A woman wearing gloves was kneeling in the dunes a few feet away. She was hunched over a seagull.

"We'll have you fixed in a jiffy," the woman said to the gull.

Alexis looked closer. The bird had a piece of plastic around its neck. It looked like a ring from a six-pack of soda.

"This seagull got its neck stuck in a plastic ring," the woman explained to Alexis. "I'm a veterinarian, and someone called to see if I could help. This bird is lucky I got here in time. It could have choked."

"That's sad," Alexis said. "I guess people need to be careful with their garbage."

"That's right," the woman said. "And it's not just gulls that get hurt. Sea turtles swallow plastic bags that are floating in the water. Seals often choke on trash, too."

Kid Power

Alexis had an idea. The next day she invited some friends over. She spread markers and cardboard on the floor and explained her plan. A few hours later the kids had made a pile of signs.

"Save a seal! Toss your trash!" read one sign.

"Snip soda rings so gulls won't choke!" read another.

Alexis and her friends got permission to post their signs on the beach. When they finished, they heard gulls crying overhead. Alexis smiled. She was certain they were saying thanks!

Building Comprehension: Reading Passages With High-Interest Practice Activities Scholastic Teaching Resources

Name ____________________ Date ____________

COMPREHENSION CHECK

Use what you learned in the story to make your way through the maze. Answer each question to choose your path. If you answer each one correctly, you will make it to the trash can!

Trash Trouble

1. The main idea of this passage is that trash ____.

A. can hurt animals

B. can often be recycled

A➤

B➤

2. The seagull in the story was hurt by a ____.

A. soup can

B. plastic six-pack ring

A➤

B➤

3. In the third paragraph the word *litter* most likely means "____."

A. garbage

B. puppy

◀A

◀B

4. Trash left on the beach most likely ____.

A. disappears on its own

B. gets into the water

A➤

B➤

5. Which sentence is a *fact* from the story?

A. Alexis is a hero.

B. Alexis makes signs.

A➤

B➤

6. In the last paragraph the word *certain* most likely means "____."

A. sure

B. kind

A➤

B➤

Write About It: What could you do to help Earth's environment and creatures? Describe three ways you could help.

Building Comprehension: Reading Passages With High-Interest Practice Activities Scholastic Teaching Resources

Name ______________________ Date ______________

NONFICTION READING PASSAGE

Before You Read: What do you know about the Olympics? When do you think the Olympic Games began?

The First Olympics

About 2,700 years ago, thousands of people gathered to watch a running race in the city of Olympia, Greece. It was the first Olympics!

The Olympics became an important Greek tradition. They were held every four years. Over time the Greeks added longer running races. They also added boxing and wrestling matches, chariot races, and two contests called the javelin and the discus.

In the javelin contest athletes competed to see who could throw a spear the farthest. In the discus contest athletes threw a round dish made of metal or wood. These sports are still in the Olympic Games today.

Strange Sports

The ancient Olympics included some unusual sports, too. In the hoplite, runners raced while carrying a shield and wearing a helmet! In the pancratium (pan-KRAY-she-um), athletes wrestled and boxed. This sport was so dangerous that athletes were sometimes killed.

In ancient Greece, Olympic winners were considered heroes. Greek poets and writers wrote about them. Artists painted pictures of them. One famous Olympic athlete was a wrestler named Milo. He rarely lost a wrestling match. Legend has it that to make himself stronger, he ran with a bull on his shoulders.

Bringing Back a Tradition

The Greeks held the Olympics for more than a thousand years. Then an emperor put an end to the games. But about one hundred years ago, a man from France decided to bring the Olympics back. Today many countries compete in the Olympic Games. The tradition that started in Greece is shared by the world.

Name ______________________ Date ______________

COMPREHENSION CHECK

Use what you learned in the story to make your way through the maze. Answer each question to choose your path. If you answer each one correctly, you will reach the finish line!

The First Olympics

1. The main idea of this passage is that the Olympic Games ____.

A. began in ancient Greece

B. are fun to watch

A➤

B➤

2. The first Olympic event was a ____.

A. running race

B. boxing match

A➤

B➤

3. *Javelin* is another word for a ____.

A. spear

B. ball

A➤

B➤

4. How do today's Olympics differ from the ancient Olympics?

A. Many nations compete.

B. There are no races.

A➤

B➤

5. In the fifth paragraph the word *match* most likely means "____."

A. contest

B. outfit

A➤

B➤

6. You can guess that the Olympic Games no longer include the ____.

A. pancratium

B. discus

A➤

B➤

FINISH!

15

Write About It: If you could be in the Olympics (ancient or modern), which event would you want to compete in? Why?

Name ______________________ Date ______________

NONFICTION READING PASSAGE

Before You Read: What do you already know about frogs and toads? Where do they live? What do they look like?

Forest Frogs Stay Safe

In a forest, rats, snakes, and other creatures often hunt frogs and toads. But many frogs and toads have ways to protect themselves. They use their skin to fool predators or scare them away.

A Disappearing Act

One way frogs and toads stay safe is to make sure they are hard to see. They use camouflage (KAM-uh-flahzh). That means they have the ability to blend in with their surroundings. For example, some frogs are bright green to match the leaves of the trees where they live. Others are brown or gold. They look like the dead leaves on the forest floor. The Asian leaf frog is one example. It easily blends in with the brown leaves on the ground. It even has ridges on its back that look like the veins on a leaf.

Some amazing frogs can even change color! They turn green when they are sitting in a tree or brown when they are sitting on the ground. That's a great way to fool a predator!

Red Alert

Other rain forest frogs and toads do not blend in at all. They have beautiful, bright colors. For example, some poison arrow frogs have blue and yellow skin. But that doesn't make them an easy target. The bright colors are a warning to rats and other enemies. The colorful frogs give off a strong poison. If a predator tries to eat the frog, it is in for a surprise. The poison can kill the predator or make it unable to move. So rats and snakes learn to stay away!

Name ______________________ Date ______________

Use what you learned in the story to make your way through the maze. Answer each question to choose your path. If you answer each one correctly, you will reach the rain forest!

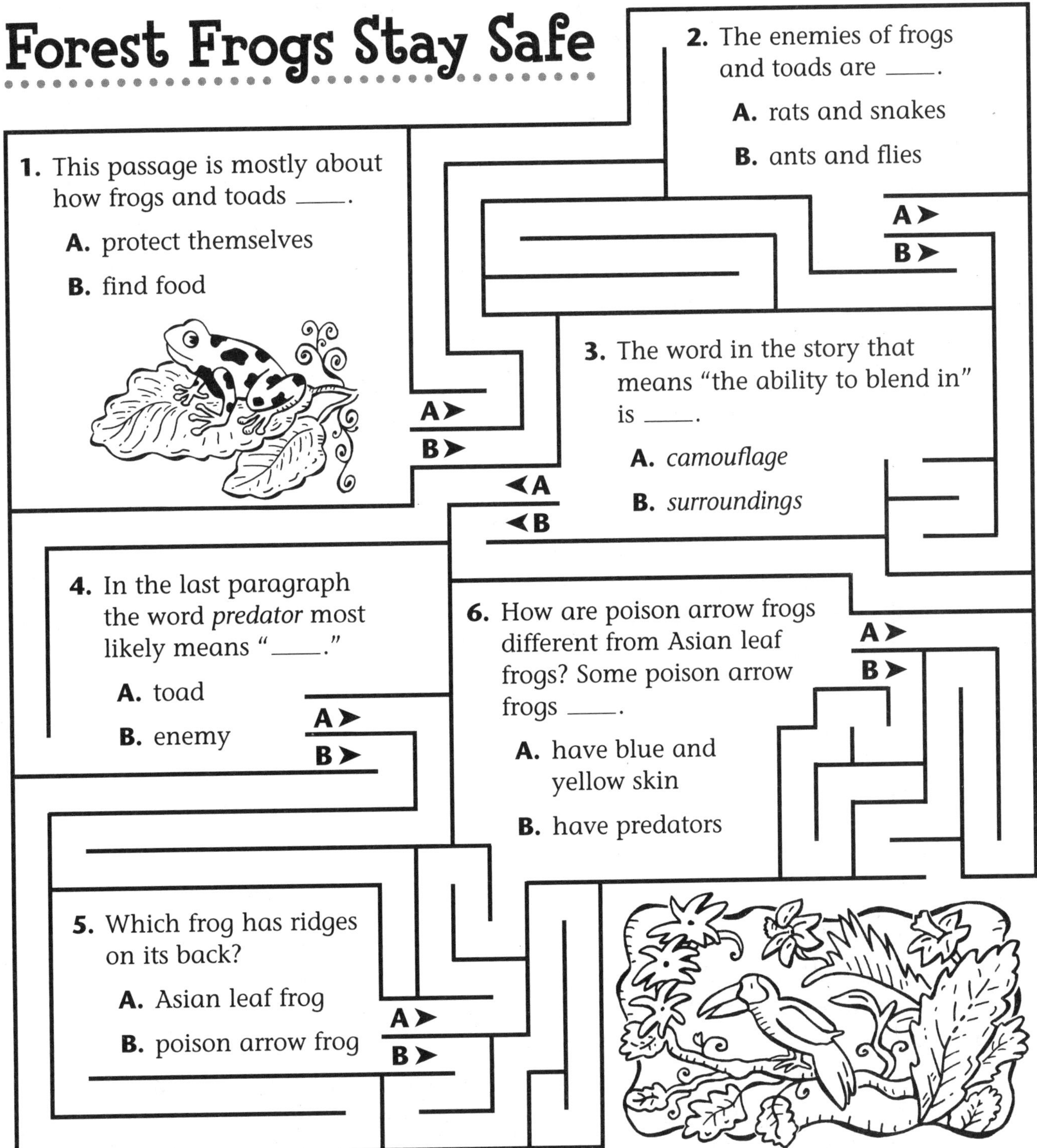

Write About It: Do you know of any other animals that have special ways of protecting themselves? Write a paragraph about one.

Name ______________________ Date ______________

NONFICTION READING PASSAGE

Before You Read: Have you ever visited a zoo? If so, what was your favorite part?

A School at the Zoo

Can you imagine going to the zoo five days a week? In Cincinnati, Ohio, some kids actually do. That's because their school is at the zoo!

The Zoo Academy is a public school that holds its classes at the Cincinnati Zoo. It opened in 1977. The academy is a special high school for students in grades 11 and 12. The teenagers who go to the school all want to work with animals when they are older.

Learning at the Zoo

Students at the Zoo Academy meet in a classroom on the zoo grounds for part of their school day. They study regular subjects such as math and social studies. But each day they also spend time learning about the animals at the zoo.

There is a lot to learn! The Cincinnati Zoo has more than 500 species of animals. Students at the academy learn by helping the zookeepers care for these creatures. For example, they feed rats to hawks and try to get penguins to take their vitamins. They clean out snake cages and help experts clean lions' teeth. Then the students take exams on their knowledge of zoo animals.

A Wild Time

Sometimes there are bad days at the Zoo Academy. For example, baby camels have chased the students. But the zookeepers make sure that students are always safe.

At graduation, the students get a fun surprise. An elephant gives out their diplomas! After graduation most students go to college to study animal science. Many of them come back to Cincinnati later to work at the zoo!

Name ______________________________ Date ________________

COMPREHENSION CHECK

A School at the Zoo

Fill in the circle next to the best answer.

1. The Zoo Academy is in ____.

○ **A.** Nevada
○ **B.** Nebraska
○ **C.** Ohio
○ **D.** Oklahoma

2. Another good title for this passage is ____.

○ **E.** "All About Snakes"
○ **F.** "A Family Trip to the Zoo"
○ **G.** "How to Feed a Hawk"
○ **H.** "Wild Lessons"

3. In the second paragraph the word *academy* probably means "____."

○ **I.** school
○ **J.** cage
○ **K.** zoo

4. Students at the Zoo Academy are in grades ____.

○ **L.** 11 and 12
○ **M.** 9 and 10
○ **N.** 7 and 8

5. Which sentence states a *fact* from the story?

○ **O.** The Cincinnati Zoo has more than 500 species of animals.
○ **P.** The Zoo Academy is an amazing place.
○ **Q.** Cleaning lions' teeth is interesting.

6. In the last paragraph the word *diplomas* most likely means "____."

○ **R.** animal tusks
○ **S.** graduation papers
○ **T.** math tests

7. How is the Zoo Academy like a regular school? Students at both schools ____.

○ **U.** clean animal cages
○ **V.** feed rats to hawks
○ **W.** brush tigers' fur
○ **X.** have math class

Now solve this riddle! Each number below stands for one of the questions. Write the letter of the correct answer above each number. You will spell out the answer to this riddle:

What kind of school has the friendliest students?

"___ ___" ___ ___ ___ ___ ___ ___!
2 3 6 1 2 5 5 4

Write About It: Would you like to attend the Zoo Academy? Why or why not? Write a paragraph supporting your point of view.

Name ______________________ Date ______________

Before You Read: Did you ever forget to do a homework assignment? If so, how did you feel?

100th Day Disaster

"Beeeeeeeeeeeeeep!"

Carly groaned as she heard her alarm clock go off. It was time to get ready for school. But Carly really wanted to stay in bed.

Carly thought about what a rotten weekend she had. On Saturday her dog had chewed her favorite pair of shoes. Then Carly accidentally spilled juice all over her family's best tablecloth. On Sunday Carly's little brother, Lewis, had forgotten to turn the faucet off in the bathroom. Water had flooded all over the place. That had put Carly's parents in very bad moods.

"At least the weekend is over," thought Carly. "Today has to be better!"

More Bad News

Carly's friend Julia called to tell her that she and her dad would be late picking up Carly for school. While they were on the phone, Carly got some bad news.

"What did you do for your 100th day project?" Julia asked.

"Oh no! I forgot!" cried Carly.

To celebrate the 100th day of the school year, Mrs. Schuster had asked students to make a poster of 100 things. Carly's stomach was in knots. She had forgotten about the project. Now she was going to be the only kid without a poster.

Quick Thinking

Carly hurried to get ready for school. While she was waiting for her ride, she came up with a plan. Carly pulled some posterboard from her desk and got to work.

At school Mrs. Schuster asked students to share their work with the class. Julia had drawn 100 butterflies. Carly presented her poster next.

"How original!" the teacher exclaimed. "Carly listed 100 things that went wrong this weekend!"

Carly decided to create a special place in her notebook to write her assignments. She was determined to have a better rest of the week!

Name ______________________ Date ______________

COMPREHENSION CHECK

100th Day Disaster

Fill in the circle next to the best answer.

1. You can guess that this story probably takes place on a ____.

○ **A.** Monday
○ **B.** Tuesday
○ **C.** Thursday

2. Carly's main problem in the story is that she ____.

○ **D.** doesn't like mornings
○ **E.** lost her backpack
○ **F.** forgot an assignment

3. You can guess that Carly probably feels ____ at the end of the story.

○ **G.** relieved
○ **H.** sad
○ **I.** scared
○ **J.** sleepy

4. In the third paragraph the word *rotten* most likely means "____."

○ **K.** wonderful
○ **L.** awful
○ **M.** relaxing
○ **N.** boring

5. How is Carly's project different from Julia's? Carly's project ____.

○ **O.** includes writing
○ **P.** includes drawings
○ **Q.** includes 100 things

6. You can predict that ____.

○ **R.** Carly will remember her homework assignments
○ **S.** Carly will get her dog a chew toy
○ **T.** Carly will get a mop

7. In the second to last paragraph the word *original* most likely means "____."

○ **U.** difficult
○ **V.** delightful
○ **W.** one of a kind

Now solve this riddle! Each number below stands for one of the questions. Write the letter of the correct answer above each number. You will spell out the answer to this riddle:

What do you put on top of a doghouse?

___	___	___	___	___!
1	7	5	5	2

Write About It: Have you ever had a really bad day? Write a short story about it. Or make up a story about an imaginary bad day!

Name ______________________ Date ______________

NONFICTION READING PASSAGE

Before You Read: Do you think April Fools' Day is an old or new holiday? How do you think it got started?

April Fools' Day

When the calendar says it's April 1, get ready for some laughs. This holiday is April Fools' Day. It is a day for telling jokes and playing funny tricks on friends. For example, one famous April Fools' joke is when a person tells a friend that his shoe is untied. When the person bends down to tie it, the joker yells, "April Fools!"

How It Started

Some historians, or history experts, believe that April Fools' Day has been around for hundreds of years. They say the holiday got its start in France back in 1582. Before that, people used to celebrate New Year's Day on April 1. But in 1582 a brand-new calendar was introduced. It was called the Gregorian calendar. On the new calendar, New Year's Day was moved to January 1. We still use this same calendar today.

Back then news traveled slowly. Many people did not hear about the new calendar right away. They kept celebrating the New Year on April 1. Other people heard about the new calendar but refused to follow it.

The First Fools

People all over France laughed at those who used the old calendar. They called them "fools" and played funny pranks on them. Before long this tradition spread throughout Europe and to other parts of the world.

Name ______________________________ Date ______________

COMPREHENSION CHECK

April Fools' Day

Fill in the circle next to the best answer.

1. A word in the last paragraph that means "tricks" is ____.

- ○ **A.** pranks
- ○ **B.** parts
- ○ **C.** calendars

2. The calendar we use today is the ____ calendar.

- ○ **D.** Greek
- ○ **E.** Gregorian
- ○ **F.** French

3. Another good title for this passage would be ____.

- ○ **G.** "Using Your Calendar"
- ○ **H.** "Jokes to Tell Your Friends"
- ○ **I.** "History of a Holiday"

4. Which of these sentences states a *fact*?

- ○ **J.** The New Year should be celebrated in April.
- ○ **K.** Pranks are always funny.
- ○ **L.** The New Year was once celebrated in April.
- ○ **M.** April Fool's Day is a lot of fun.

5. You can guess that news about the calendar change probably traveled slowly because ____.

- ○ **N.** the people who made the change forgot to tell people
- ○ **O.** cell phone service was bad back then
- ○ **P.** there were no cars or phones to help spread the news
- ○ **Q.** some people wanted to keep it a secret

6. In the first paragraph the word *famous* most likely means "____."

- ○ **R.** well-known
- ○ **S.** brand-new
- ○ **T.** different

Now solve this riddle! Each number below stands for one of the questions. Write the letter of the correct answer above each number. You will spell out the answer to this riddle:

What kind of fruit is never alone?

____   ____ ____ ____ ____!
1   5 2 1 6

Write About It: Write a paragraph about the funniest April Fools' joke you have ever experienced.

Name ______________________ Date ______________________

Before You Read: Have you ever heard of Aesop's fables? What do you think they are?

The Ant and the Dove

A fable is an old story that teaches a moral, or lesson. In a fable, animals talk and act like humans. Here's a fable about an ant and a dove.

A Big Splash

Once, a tiny ant built its home in a forest. The hard work made Ant thirsty, so he set out in search of a cool drink.

Soon Ant arrived at a river. He crawled to the water's edge and leaned down to take a sip. But the water was too far away, so Ant had to crawl closer. This time he got a mouthful of cool, clear water.

"Delicious!" thought Ant. But before he could take a second sip, Ant began to slide into the river. He fell into the water and was carried along in the stream.

A Feathered Friend

Luckily, a kind dove was flying over the river and saw that Ant was in trouble. She looked around for a way to assist him. Dove spotted a small twig on the ground. She swooped down and picked up the twig in her sharp beak. Then she dropped it into the river near Ant. Grateful Ant climbed onto the twig. He rode it until the twig was washed onto the banks of the river.

Later Ant was out looking for food when he saw Dove again. Dove was flying high above the treetops.

"That's the dove that saved my life," Ant thought. Then Ant spotted a hunter with a weapon aimed at Dove. He knew he had to help his friend. Thinking quickly, Ant hurried to the hunter and stung him on the foot.

The surprised hunter dropped his weapon and leaned down to rub his foot. Tiny Ant had repaid Dove's favor.

Name ______________________________ Date ____________________

The Ant and the Dove

Fill in the circle next to the best answer.

1. A fable is a story with a ____.

○ **A.** lesson
○ **B.** happy ending
○ **C.** princess

2. In this fable Ant sets out to ____.

○ **D.** cross the river
○ **E.** get a drink of water
○ **F.** make a friend
○ **G.** go swimming

3. A word in the fifth paragraph that means "nice" is ____.

○ **H.** grateful
○ **I.** kind
○ **J.** sharp
○ **K.** close

4. Another good title for this passage would be ____.

○ **L.** "A Giant Anthill"
○ **M.** "Forest Friends"
○ **N.** "Water Safety"

5. Dove helps Ant by ____.

○ **O.** dropping a twig into the water
○ **P.** building an anthill
○ **Q.** telling him where to find the river

6. In the fifth paragraph the word *assist* most likely means "____."

○ **R.** help
○ **S.** know
○ **T.** see

7. At the end of the story, you can predict that Dove will probably ____.

○ **U.** fall in the river
○ **V.** fly away safely
○ **W.** chase the hunter

8. The moral of this fable is most likely that ____.

○ **X.** no one should waste time
○ **Y.** anyone can be a helpful friend
○ **Z.** honesty is important

Now solve this riddle! Each number below stands for one of the questions. Write the letter of the correct answer above each number. You will spell out the answer to this riddle:

What has a mouth but cannot smile?

___ ___ ___ ___ ___ ___!
1 6 3 7 2 6

Write About It: Write your own fable! Include animals that can talk and an important lesson.

Name ______________________ Date ______________

NONFICTION READING PASSAGE

Before You Read: What is a fossil? Can you give some examples of fossils?

A Dino Discovery

In the summer of 1996, Fernando Novas was hard at work in Argentina. Novas is a paleontologist, a scientist who studies fossils. He was digging through the rocky earth, looking for dinosaur bones.

After many weeks Novas made an exciting find. It was a huge dinosaur claw! The claw was razor sharp and more than a foot long. As Novas and his team studied the fossil, they realized that they had made an amazing discovery. The claw belonged to a new kind of dinosaur. They decided to name the dino Megaraptor. That name means "giant thief."

A Big Beast

The claw and other fossils gave Novas some clues about the Megaraptor. He estimated that the Megaraptor was probably about 25 feet long and weighed about 1½ tons. Its large, scary claws made it one of the fiercest dinos that ever lived. It used its claws to hunt for food.

The Megaraptor claw was found in southern Argentina. This area is called Patagonia (pat-uh-GO-nee-uh). It is a rocky desert area with hot, dry summers and windy, cold winters. But scientists say that millions of years ago, Patagonia was a steamy jungle. Back then it was home to some of the world's biggest dinosaurs.

A Dino Hot Spot

The Megaraptor is not the only big beast that lived in Patagonia. Scientists have also found fossils from the Giganotosaurus and the Argentinosaurus. Giganotosaurus was a meat-eater. It weighed eight tons. Argentinosaurus was even bigger. It was a plant-eater that weighed up to 100 tons!

Since the late 1990s scientists have continued digging for dino fossils in southern Argentina. It's one of the world's dino hot spots!

Name ______________________________ Date ____________________

COMPREHENSION CHECK

A Dino Discovery

Fill in the circle next to the best answer.

1. Another good title for this passage might be ____.

- ○ **A.** "Dinosaur Fossils"
- ○ **B.** "What Scientists Do"
- ○ **C.** "Swamp Life"

2. A paleontologist is a scientist who studies ____.

- ○ **D.** deserts
- ○ **E.** fossils

3. Which of these sentences states an *opinion*?

- ○ **F.** Paleontologists have exciting jobs.
- ○ **G.** Fernando Novas is a paleontologist.
- ○ **H.** Novas found a long, sharp claw.

4. You can guess that Megaraptor was most likely a ____.

- ○ **I.** gentle dinosaur
- ○ **J.** type of bird
- ○ **K.** plant-eater
- ○ **L.** meat-eater

5. How were Giganotosaurus and Argentinosaurus different? Giganotosaurus was ____.

- ○ **M.** smaller
- ○ **N.** larger
- ○ **O.** faster
- ○ **P.** slower

6. In the fifth paragraph the word *beast* most likely means "____."

- ○ **Q.** fish
- ○ **R.** monster
- ○ **S.** bird
- ○ **T.** animal

7. The Megaraptor most likely lived ____.

- ○ **U.** hundreds of years ago
- ○ **V.** thousands of years ago
- ○ **W.** millions of years ago

8. Today Patagonia is a ____.

- ○ **X.** rocky desert
- ○ **Y.** steamy jungle
- ○ **Z.** dinosaur museum

Now solve this riddle! Each number below stands for one of the questions. Write the letter of the correct answer above each number. You will spell out the answer to this riddle:

What kind of dinosaur likes to work out?

___ ___. ___ ___ ___ ___
1 6 3 4 2 8

Write About It: Imagine that you are a scientist and have just discovered a new kind of dinosaur. Name it and describe what you think it would have looked like.

Name ________________________ Date ________________

Before You Read: Is winning important to you? Why or why not?

We All Win!

Aliya was having a problem with her friend Laura. The trouble was that Laura turned everything into a contest.

Winning Ways

In February Aliya had brought balloons to school for her birthday. Laura took one and said, "Look! My balloon is the biggest!"

One day in March Aliya and Laura had both worn purple shirts. They did not plan it that way. But Laura had asked everyone, "Whose shirt do you think is prettier?"

In April the class had taken a tour of the post office. When the students made a thank-you note for the postmaster, Laura spent five whole minutes signing her name. Then she told everyone that she had the most elegant handwriting in the whole class. That made Aliya feel bad. She was still learning to write her name in cursive.

Playing with Laura was getting to be a challenge. If you asked her to play ball, she would immediately compete to see who could throw the ball the farthest. If you asked her to play Go Fish, she would keep starting over until she had the best cards.

One day after school Laura was finding a seat on the bus.

"I've got the best seat!" she called out.

No Contest

Aliya was sitting nearby. She decided to tell her friend what was bothering her. "Laura, I don't want to compete with you—you're my friend," she explained.

"I'm sorry," Laura said. "I'll work on it. Is it all right if we have one last contest?"

"Well, I guess so," said Aliya.

"Here it is," said Laura. "Let's see who can go the longest without competing!"

Name ______________________ Date ______________

We All Win!

Fill in the circle next to the best answer.

1. In the story Laura likes to ____.

- ○ **A.** compete
- ○ **B.** argue

2. What is one way that Aliya and Laura are alike?

- ○ **C.** Both girls have purple shirts.
- ○ **D.** Both girls brought balloons to school.
- ○ **E.** Both girls like to compete.
- ○ **F.** Both girls have birthdays in February.

3. What is one way that Aliya and Laura are different? Aliya ____.

- ○ **G.** rides the bus
- ○ **H.** visited the post office
- ○ **I.** has a birthday in February

4. In the fourth paragraph the word *elegant* probably means "____."

- ○ **J.** large
- ○ **K.** plain
- ○ **L.** fancy

5. In the fifth paragraph the word *immediately* probably means "____."

- ○ **M.** never
- ○ **N.** right away
- ○ **O.** soon

6. At the end of the story, you can guess that Laura ____.

- ○ **P.** will try to stop competing
- ○ **Q.** will ask Aliya to sit with her on the bus

7. Which sentence states an *opinion*?

- ○ **R.** Cursive writing is fun.
- ○ **S.** Aliya and Laura are in the same class.
- ○ **T.** Aliya and Laura ride the bus.

Now solve this riddle! Each number below stands for one of the questions. Write the letter of the correct answer above each number. You will spell out the answer to this riddle:

What do you call a friend at school?

The ___ ___ ___ ___ ___ ___-___ ___ ___!
6 7 3 5 2 3 6 1 4

Write About It: What would you say to a friend who is sad that he or she had lost a big game?

Name ______________________ Date ______________

NONFICTION READING PASSAGE

Before You Read: How would you define music? What are some things people can use to make music?

They Have the Beat!

Most bands make music the traditional way. They play pianos, drums, guitars, and other instruments. Not Stomp! Stomp is a musical group with eight members. They do not use regular instruments. Instead, they make music using everyday objects like broomsticks, garbage cans, water bottles, and basketballs.

How Stomp Started

Two men created Stomp more than ten years ago. They began performing on the streets of England. They would stomp their feet and bang broomsticks together to create a lively beat. People would stop to watch the musicians. Some would give their extra change to the performers to show that they enjoyed the music.

The two men added other members to their group. Soon they were putting on shows in theaters and earning a living by making music. Today Stomp performs in dozens of cities each year. The group travels all over the globe to share its one-of-a-kind music.

A Fun Show

During a Stomp show, the performers wear heavy boots or clogs. That helps them make plenty of noise when they stomp their feet. They also bang on trash cans, bounce balls, crackle newspapers, and hit empty water jugs. Together, the strange sounds make a catchy rhythm.

Audience members watch the performers stomp, spin, jump, and dance. Then Stomp invites the crowd to clap and stomp along. The audience loves it!

Banging broomsticks and stomping your feet might sound easy, but it's not! The Stomp musicians practice hard to get their music just right. With all that stomping, they get more than their fair share of ankle aches and broken toes. And they go through a lot of instruments. They use more than 85 brooms in a month!

Name ______________________ Date ______________

They Have the Beat!

Work with a partner on this tic-tac-toe game. Here's how:

1. Each player chooses a different crayon.
2. Players take turns choosing any box on the board. Answer the question in your box. Then color the box with your crayon.
3. When all the questions have been answered, check your answers with an answer key. The object is to get three correct answers in a row (across, down, or diagonally).

1. Another good title for this passage is ____. ○ **A.** "Stomp's Special Sound" ○ **B.** "An Amazing Sight"	**2.** How is Stomp different from other musical groups? Stomp ____. ○ **A.** does not play in theaters ○ **B.** does not use traditional instruments	**3.** Stomp members would probably *not* make music with a ____. ○ **A.** bucket ○ **B.** saxophone
4. Stomp members wear ____. ○ **A.** slippers or sneakers ○ **B.** clogs or boots	**5.** Complete this sentence to state a *fact*. Stomp ____. ○ **A.** has eight members ○ **B.** is a great band	**6.** You can guess from the story that Stomp performs only in England. ○ **A.** true ○ **B.** false
7. In the last paragraph the word *aches* most likely means "____." ○ **A.** breaks ○ **B.** pains	**8.** This passage is mainly about ____. ○ **A.** an unusual band ○ **B.** how to play instruments	**9.** Why does Stomp use so many brooms? It's most likely because ____. ○ **A.** brooms break during shows ○ **B.** audience members take brooms home

Write About It: Imagine that Stomp is coming to perform in your town. Write a newspaper or magazine advertisement to get people interested in seeing the show.

Name ______________________ Date ______________

Before You Read: If you could give your best friend a present, what would it be?

The Friendship Box

The holidays were coming, and Danielle had a problem. She did not have a gift for her friend Roger. She and Roger had been buddies since preschool. Now Roger had invited Danielle to see his sister's dance recital with his family. Danielle loved to watch dance. She wanted to give Roger his present at the theater. But she had only two days to come up with a gift!

Danielle knew that Roger would like a book about snakes or a board game. But she did not have enough money to purchase either one.

Looking for Ideas

Danielle looked through her mom's catalogs for ideas. She smiled when she saw a photo of kids riding bikes. That was one of the things she and Roger both loved to do. In another catalog, Danielle saw an ad for art supplies. Roger loved to draw.

"I'm just wasting time," thought Danielle. "I don't have enough money to buy these things."

Suddenly, Danielle's eyes lit up. The catalogs had given her an idea. She grabbed some scissors and cut out the two pictures. Then she found other pictures that reminded her of Roger. Finally, she went to find a shoe box in her closet.

Putting It All Together

Danielle pasted the pictures onto the box. Then she wrote a brief poem to put inside. It said, "I didn't get you a book or a game. But you are my best friend all the same!"

On Saturday Danielle and Roger went to the dance recital. Afterward Danielle gave Roger his gift.

"Wow!" Roger exclaimed. "It's a box covered with all my favorite things."

Name ______________________ Date ______________

The Friendship Box

Work with a partner on this tic-tac-toe game. Here's how:

1. Each player chooses a different crayon.
2. Players take turns choosing any box on the board. Answer the question in your box. Then color the box with your crayon.
3. When all the questions have been answered, check your answers with an answer key. The object is to get three correct answers in a row (across, down, or diagonally).

1. In the story Danielle wants to get her friend a ____. ○ **A.** birthday card ○ **B.** holiday gift	**2.** You can guess from the story that Roger ____. ○ **A.** liked the gift ○ **B.** planned to store art supplies in it	**3.** In the second paragraph the word *purchase* probably means ____. ○ **A.** find ○ **B.** buy
4. To get gift ideas, Danielle looks at ____. ○ **A.** television ads ○ **B.** catalogs	**5.** How are Roger and Danielle alike? They both ____. ○ **A.** make a friendship box ○ **B.** like to ride bikes	**6.** Danielle knew that Roger would like a book about ____. ○ **A.** snakes ○ **B.** hockey
7. In the sixth paragraph the word *brief* most likely means "____." ○ **A.** strange ○ **B.** short	**8.** This passage is mainly about ____. ○ **A.** a friend trying to find the right gift ○ **B.** two friends sharing memories	**9.** Review the end of the story. What will Roger most likely say next? ○ **A.** "Do you have your ticket?" ○ **B.** "Thank you!"

Write About It: Imagine that you are going to make a friendship box for someone you know. What kinds of pictures would you put on it? Why?

Name ____________________ Date ____________________

NONFICTION READING PASSAGE

Before You Read: What do you do with fruit peels and other scraps of food?

Garbage in the Garden

Did you know that a banana peel can help a garden grow? Food scraps like banana peels, bread crusts, and apple cores have ingredients that can help plants grow fast and strong. These scraps can be used to make compost. Compost is a rich soil that can be spread in a garden or put in the pots of houseplants. Here's how to make it:

1. **Pick a place:** Choose a spot outdoors for your compost heap. If you have a garden, the pile should be close to it. You might create your compost in a container.
2. **Collect dead leaves.** Put a layer of dead leaves in your compost spot. Sprinkle water on top of the leaves.
3. **Add food scraps:** Put food scraps and grass clippings on top of the leaves. Toss in fruit and vegetable scraps, bread crusts, and coffee grounds. (Don't use meat scraps. Meat will smell bad after a few days and may attract animals.) Sprinkle more water on the compost heap.
4. **Add dirt:** Put a layer of soil on top of the heap. The soil has tiny living things in it. You can't see them, but they will help turn your trash into compost. Turn over the pile every once in a while.
5. **Watch it work:** After a few weeks you will notice changes in your compost heap. It will be dark and warm. It may also have earthworms. These are signs that the compost heap is working! The tiny living things are helping the scraps decompose, or break down.
6. **Spread the compost:** Use a shovel to spread compost around your garden. You can also put it in houseplants. Finally, watch your plants grow!

If you would like to make a compost heap, ask for permission first. Then watch your plants grow strong and healthy!

Name ______________________ Date ______________

Garbage in the Garden

Work with a partner on this tic-tac-toe game. Here's how:

1. Each player chooses a different crayon.
2. Players take turns choosing any box on the board. Answer the question in your box. Then color the box with your crayon.
3. When all the questions have been answered, check your answers with an answer key. The object is to get three correct answers in a row (across, down, or diagonally).

1. Another good title for this passage is ____. ○ **A.** "Don't Pollute" ○ **B.** "Making Compost"	**2.** Compost is a type of ____. ○ **A.** soil ○ **B.** plant	**3.** Bread crusts and ____ can both be used in a compost pile. ○ **A.** meat scraps ○ **B.** apple cores
4. The first thing you should put in a compost heap is ____. ○ **A.** dead leaves ○ **B.** water	**5.** In the first step the word *heap* probably means "____." ○ **A.** trash ○ **B.** pile	**6.** You can guess from the story that if you see worms in your pile, the compost is ruined. ○ **A.** true ○ **B.** false
7. Is this statement a fact or opinion? "Everyone should have a compost pile." ○ **A.** fact ○ **B.** opinion	**8.** You can predict that once you add compost to your garden, the plants will probably ____. ○ **A.** grow strong and healthy ○ **B.** need less sun	**9.** In the fifth step the word *decompose* means "____." ○ **A.** to throw away ○ **B.** to break down

Write About It: Making compost is one way you can help nature. What other ways can you think of? Make a list of five things.

Name ______________________ Date ______________

Before You Read: Do you like to watch television? Why or why not?

Too Much TV

Duncan ran into the house and headed for the TV. It was time for his favorite show, Zappy-Zippers.

"Oops!" Duncan said to himself as he reached for the remote. "I almost forgot about the TV-Free Challenge!"

The TV-Free Challenge was a project at Duncan's school. His teacher, Mr. Green, had challenged the kids and their families to turn off their TVs for one week. That meant no cartoons, no movies—and no Zappy-Zippers.

Time for Fun

Duncan knew he probably watched too much TV. Last month his class had kept TV logs. They had written down every show they watched. Duncan discovered that he sometimes watched more than two hours of television a day!

Now it was time to do something else. Duncan decided to play fetch with his dog. After dinner he did homework and played a card game with his mom.

For the next few days, Duncan kept busy. He went to soccer practice and read books. He taught his little sister to tie her shoes.

On Friday Duncan's mom forgot about the TV-Free Challenge. She turned on the TV to watch the news, but then Duncan reminded her.

A Job Well Done

On Monday the challenge was over. Mr. Green gave the students awards for doing the project. Duncan couldn't wait to show his family. When he got home, he saw that his dad was preparing dinner. Duncan showed him his award. Then he put on an apron to help.

When they had finished, Duncan glanced at the clock. It was almost 5:30.

"Guess what, Dad," he said. "I forgot all about Zappy-Zippers. And I didn't even miss it!"

Name ______________________ Date ______________

Too Much TV

Work with a partner on this tic-tac-toe game. Here's how:

1. Each player chooses a different crayon.
2. Players take turns choosing any box on the board. Answer the question in your box. Then color the box with your crayon.
3. When all the questions have been answered, check your answers with an answer key. The object is to get three correct answers in a row (across, down, or diagonally).

1. Duncan's goal is to go one week without ____. ○ **A.** junk food ○ **B.** television	**2.** In the fourth paragraph the word *logs* probably means "____." ○ **A.** trees ○ **B.** journals	**3.** Duncan taught his little sister to ____. ○ **A.** tie her shoes ○ **B.** play cards
4. You can tell that Duncan was ____ during the TV-Free Challenge. ○ **A.** busy ○ **B.** bored	**5.** You can guess from the story that Duncan is probably on a ____ team. ○ **A.** baseball ○ **B.** soccer	**6.** Duncan's ____ forgets about the challenge and turns on the TV. ○ **A.** mom ○ **B.** sister
7. You can predict that Duncan will probably ____. ○ **A.** watch two hours of TV a day ○ **B.** watch less TV from now on	**8.** Complete this sentence to state a *fact*. The TV-Free Challenge ____. ○ **A.** lasted one week ○ **B.** was a fantastic idea	**9.** In the ninth paragraph the word *glanced* means "____." ○ **A.** smiled ○ **B.** looked

Write About It: If you didn't watch TV for a week, what are some of the things you might do instead?

Name ______________________________ Date ____________________

FICTION READING PASSAGE

Before You Read: Have you ever been to a carnival or fair? What was it like?

Finding Freddy

"What will it be?" the man at the snack counter asked. Meg asked for a small bag of popcorn. She gave her brother, Freddy, a handful of popcorn and put the rest of the bag in her backpack.

Sights and Sounds

The Wilsons strolled around the carnival grounds. They stopped to have their picture taken in a little booth. Meg and Freddy both made funny faces in the photo. Mrs. Wilson laughed when the picture came out of the machine.

As they walked, Freddy asked to go on all the rides. He especially liked the enormous Ferris wheel.

"Okay, okay," Mrs. Wilson said. She got in line to buy some ride tickets. While they waited in line, Meg reached into her backpack to grab some more popcorn. It had disappeared—and so had Freddy!

Crunchy Clues

Meg and her mom searched frantically. The ticket seller offered to help, too.

"What does Freddy look like?" the woman asked.

Meg remembered the funny photo and went to get it from her bag. But as she looked at the ground, she noticed a trail of popcorn.

"I think Freddy went this way!" she yelled.

Meg and her mom followed the trail. It led to the line for the Ferris wheel. Meg looked at the long line. There was Freddy! He was standing in line and munching on the last few pieces of popcorn.

As Mrs. Wilson hugged Freddy, she reminded him never to wander off. Then she thanked Meg for her detective work.

"No problem!" said Meg. "But playing detective did make me hungry. Can we get a refill?"

Name ____________________ Date ____________

Finding Freddy

Work with a partner on this tic-tac-toe game. Here's how:

1. Each player chooses a different crayon.
2. Players take turns choosing any box on the board. Answer the question in your box. Then color the box with your crayon.
3. When all the questions have been answered, check your answers with an answer key. The object is to get three correct answers in a row (across, down, or diagonally).

1. This passage is mainly about a girl who is trying to ____.

○ **A.** choose a healthy snack

○ **B.** find her brother

2. In the second paragraph the word *strolled* probably means "____."

○ **A.** walked

○ **B.** danced

3. You can tell that Freddy is probably ____ than Meg.

○ **A.** younger

○ **B.** older

4. Does this sentence state a fact or opinion? "The carnival is more fun than the zoo."

○ **A.** fact

○ **B.** opinion

5. Mrs. Wilson and Meg find Freddy ____.

○ **A.** at the snack counter

○ **B.** in line for the Ferris wheel

6. In the third paragraph the word *enormous* most likely means "____."

○ **A.** colorful

○ **B.** huge

7. A trail of ____ leads Meg to Freddy.

○ **A.** footprints

○ **B.** popcorn

8. At the end of the story, you can guess that Meg feels ____.

○ **A.** sad

○ **B.** relieved

9. What do you predict the Wilsons will do next? They will probably ____.

○ **A.** get more popcorn

○ **B.** get a picture taken

Write About It: What are your family's safety rules when you are outside your home or in a crowded place? What does your family tell you to do if you get lost?

Name ______________________ Date ______________________

NONFICTION READING PASSAGE

Before You Read: What are some things you use to stay warm in winter?

A Cool Inventor

One winter day in 1873, a teenager named Chester Greenwood was ice-skating near his home. Chester lived in Farmington, Maine, and the winters there were freezing cold. Chester wanted to keep skating, but his ears were getting very cold. He tried wrapping his scarf around his head. But the scarf was too bulky. Chester thought a hat would be too itchy, and he did not like the way hats looked.

A Warm Solution

Back home Chester tried to imagine other ways to keep ears warm in winter. He finally came up with a perfect idea. He made two round loops from wire and asked his grandmother to sew fur on them. Then he added a steel band to hold the two loops in place. It was the first pair of earmuffs!

Chester was only 15 years old. But that didn't stop him from turning his invention into a big success. He named his invention Greenwood's Champion Ear Protectors. He opened a factory to make his earmuffs. Many Americans bought the new invention.

When Chester grew up, he invented about a hundred other things, including one of the first garden rakes. But earmuffs were still his most famous—and most popular—invention.

Making It Big

When Chester was 56 years old, the United States went to war. American soldiers were fighting in Europe. The army needed something to shield soldiers' ears from the cold. It bought earmuffs from Chester Greenwood for all of its soldiers.

Today the town of Farmington, Maine, still remembers Chester Greenwood. They even have a parade every December on his birthday!

Name ______________________ Date ______________

A Cool Inventor

Work with a partner on this tic-tac-toe game. Here's how:

1. Each player chooses a different crayon.
2. Players take turns choosing any box on the board. Answer the question in your box. Then color the box with your crayon.
3. When all the questions have been answered, check your answers with an answer key. The object is to get three correct answers in a row (across, down, or diagonally).

1. This story is mainly about ____. ○ **A.** an inventor ○ **B.** staying warm	**2.** Chester invented earmuffs because he ____. ○ **A.** was cold ○ **B.** liked hats	**3.** Chester invented earmuffs when he was ____. ○ **A.** 18 years old ○ **B.** 15 years old
4. In the second paragraph the word *imagine* most likely means "____." ○ **A.** to think of ○ **B.** to describe	**5.** You can guess that Chester Greenwood ____. ○ **A.** was successful ○ **B.** joined the army	**6.** In the fifth paragraph the word *shield* most likely means "____." ○ **A.** to protect ○ **B.** to plug
7. How many things did Chester invent? ○ **A.** only earmuffs ○ **B.** about a hundred	**8.** Chester also invented one of the first ____. ○ **A.** garden rakes ○ **B.** telephones	**9.** You can guess that the people of Farmington, Maine, ____. ○ **A.** are proud of Chester Greenwood ○ **B.** buy a lot of earmuffs

Write About It: What do you think is the world's most useful invention? Why?

Answer Key

CROSSWORD PUZZLES

Pages 18–19 (Feeling Hot, Hot, Hot)
Across 4. B; 6. A; 7. B; 8. A; Down 1. A; 2. B; 3. B; 5. A

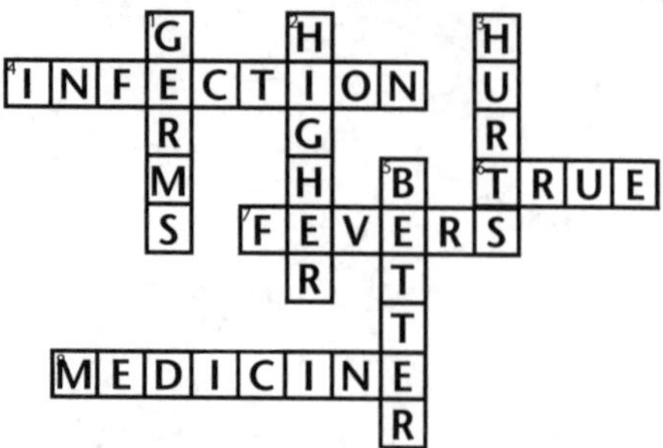

Pages 20–21 (Teddy's Story)
Across 2. B; 5. B; 7. B; 8. B; Down 1. A; 3. B; 4. A; 6. A

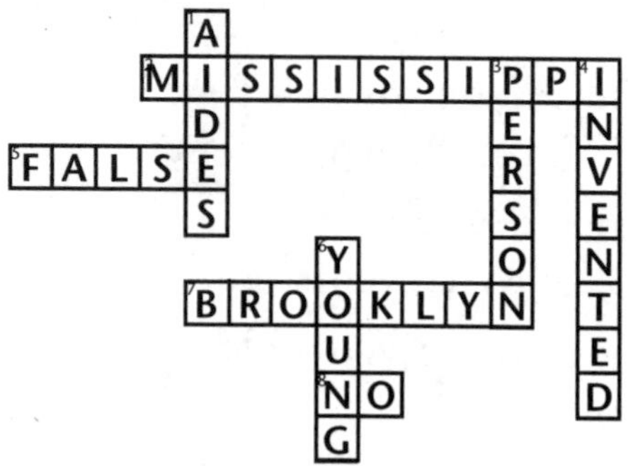

Pages 22–23 (The Great Barrier Reef)
Across 1. A; 5. B; 6. B; 8. B; Down 2. B; 3. A; 4. A; 7. A

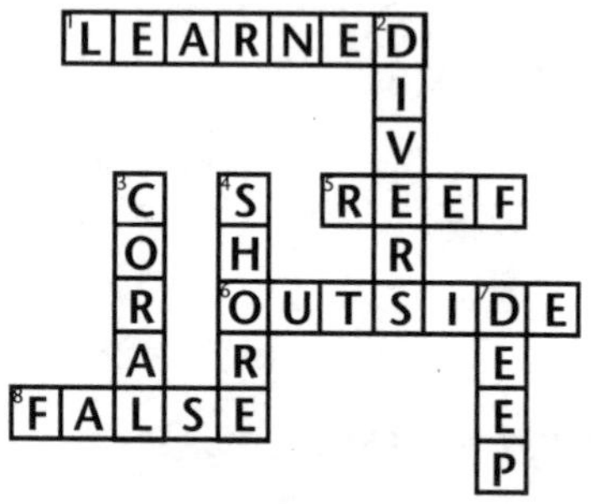

Pages 24–25 (A Day at the Zoo)
Across 3. B; 5. A; 7. A; 8. B; Down 1. B; 2. B; 4. A; 6. B

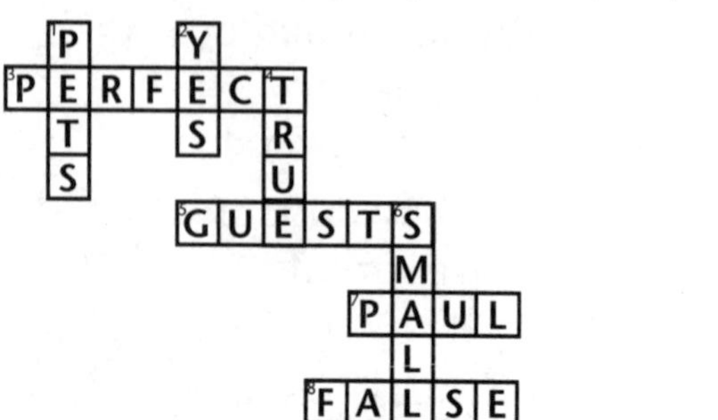

Pages 26–27 (A Cool Hotel!)
Across 2. A; 4. B; 5. A; 6. B; 7. B; Down 1. B; 3. A; 6. A

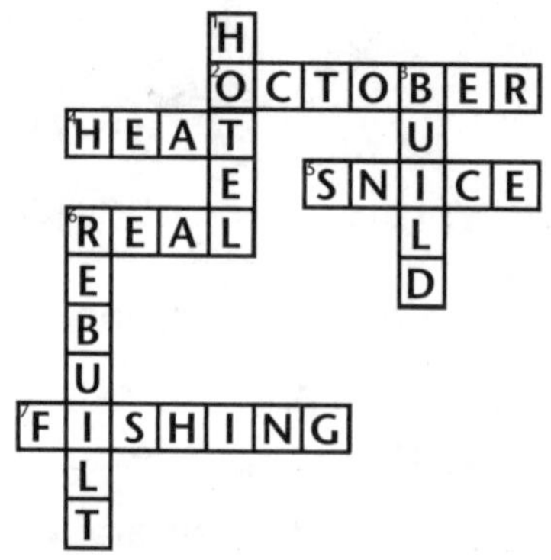

Pages 28–29 (The Sleepover)
Across 3. B; 5. A; 6. A; 7. B; Down 1. B; 2. A; 4. A; 8. A

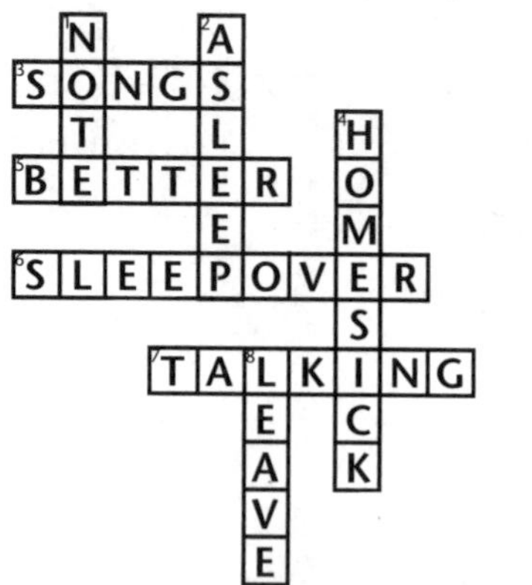

WORD SEARCHES

Pages 30–31 (The Sinking City)
1. A; 2. B; 3. B; 4. A; 5. B; 6. B; 7. B; 8. A

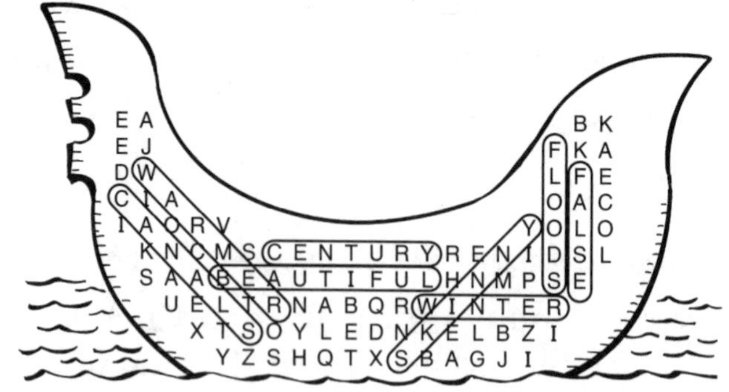

Pages 32–33 (Horrible Hiccups)
1. A; 2. A; 3. B; 4. B; 5. A; 6. B; 7. B

Pages 34–35 (Why Leaves Change Color)

1. B; 2. B; 3. A; 4. A; 5. B; 6. B; 7. B; 8. A

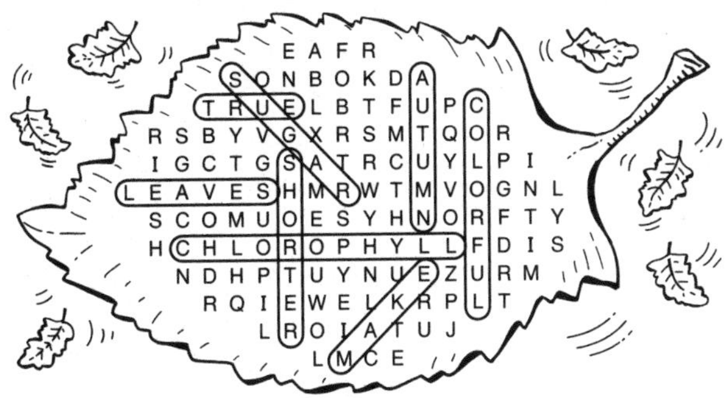

Pages 36–37 (Paul Bunyan)

1. B; 2. A; 3. A; 4. A; 5. B; 6. A; 7. B

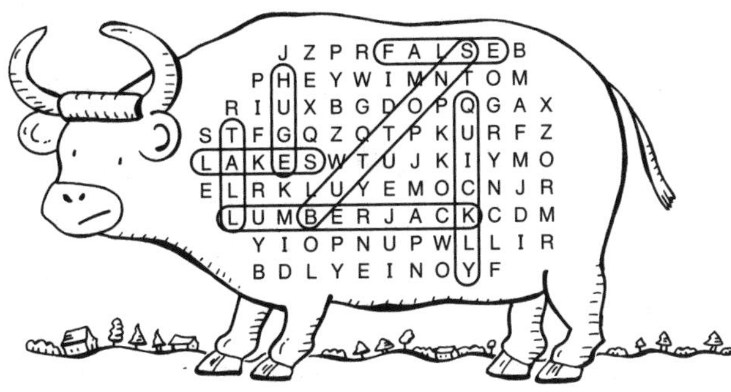

Pages 38–39 (Lily on the Loose)

1. A; 2. B; 3. A; 4. A; 5. B; 6. A; 7. A; 8. A

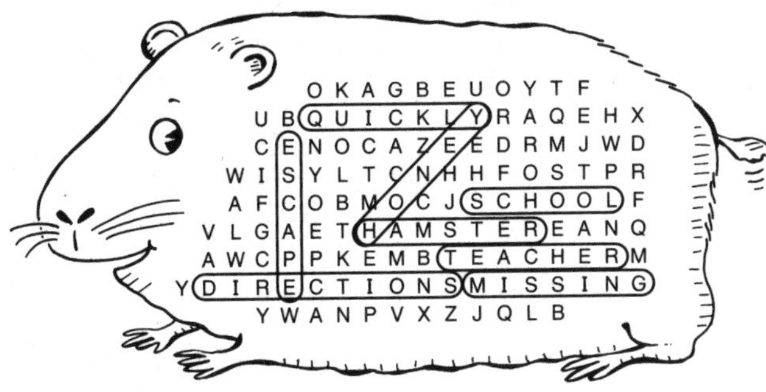

Pages 40–41 (Trunk Talk)

1. B; 2. B; 3. A; 4. B; 5. A; 6. B; 7. B; 8. B

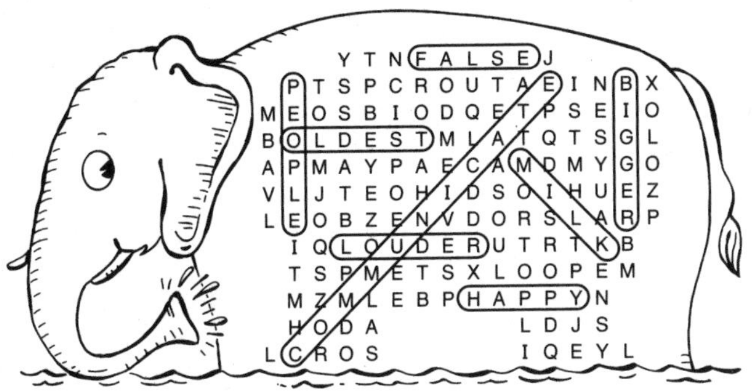

COMPREHENSION MAZES

Pages 42–43 (Vitamin ABCs)

1. A; 2. A; 3. A; 4. A; 5. B; 6. B

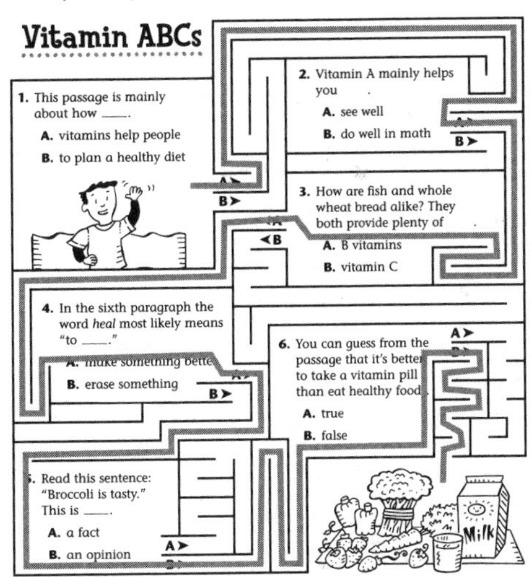
Vitamin ABCs
1. This passage is mainly about how ___.
A. vitamins help people
B. to plan a healthy diet
2. Vitamin A mainly helps you ___.
A. see well
B. do well in math
3. How are fish and whole wheat bread alike? They both provide plenty of ___.
A. B vitamins
B. vitamin C
4. In the sixth paragraph the word heal most likely means "to ___."
B. erase something
6. You can guess from the passage that it's better to take a vitamin pill than eat healthy food.
A. true
B. false
5. Read this sentence: "Broccoli is tasty." This is ___.
A. a fact
B. an opinion
Milk

Pages 44–45 (Happy New Year!)

1. A; 2. A; 3. B; 4. A; 5. A; 6. B

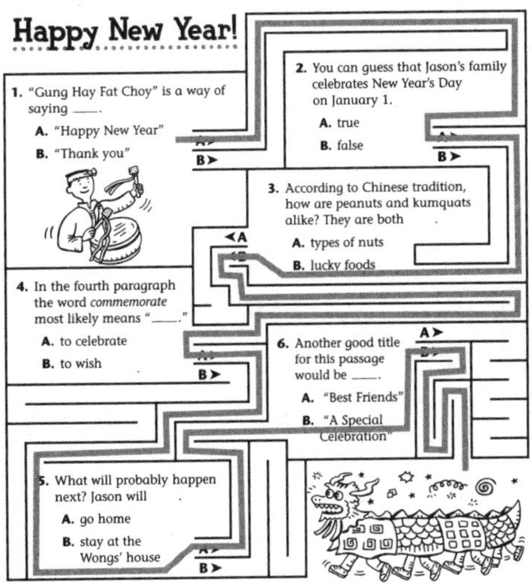
Happy New Year!
1. "Gung Hay Fat Choy" is a way of saying ___.
A. "Happy New Year"
B. "Thank you"
2. You can guess that Jason's family celebrates New Year's Day on January 1.
A. true
B. false
3. According to Chinese tradition, how are peanuts and kumquats alike? They are both ___.
A. types of nuts
B. lucky foods
4. In the fourth paragraph the word commemorate most likely means "___."
A. to celebrate
B. to wish
6. Another good title for this passage would be ___.
A. "Best Friends"
B. "A Special Celebration"
5. What will probably happen next? Jason will ___.
A. go home
B. stay at the Wongs' house

Pages 46–47 (Animal Pals)

1. B; 2. A; 3. B; 4. B; 5. B; 6. A

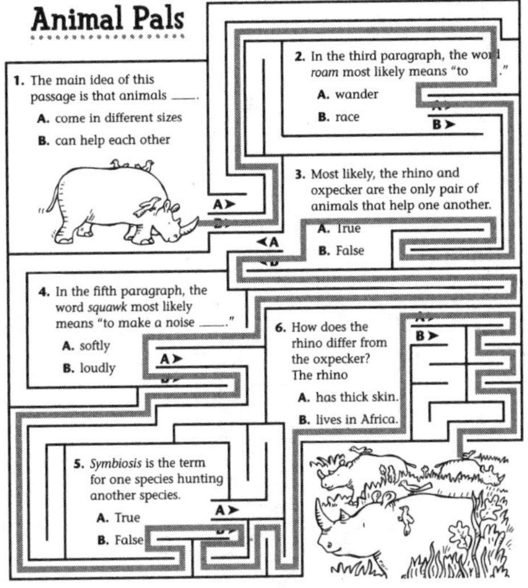
Animal Pals
1. The main idea of this passage is that animals ___.
A. come in different sizes
B. can help each other
2. In the third paragraph, the word roam most likely means "to ___."
A. wander
B. race
3. Most likely, the rhino and oxpecker are the only pair of animals that help one another.
A. True
B. False
4. In the fifth paragraph, the word squawk most likely means "to make a noise ___."
A. softly
B. loudly
6. How does the rhino differ from the oxpecker? The rhino ___.
A. has thick skin.
B. lives in Africa.
5. Symbiosis is the term for one species hunting another species.
A. True
B. False

Pages 48–49 (Trash Trouble)
1. A; 2. B; 3. A; 4. B; 5. B; 6. A

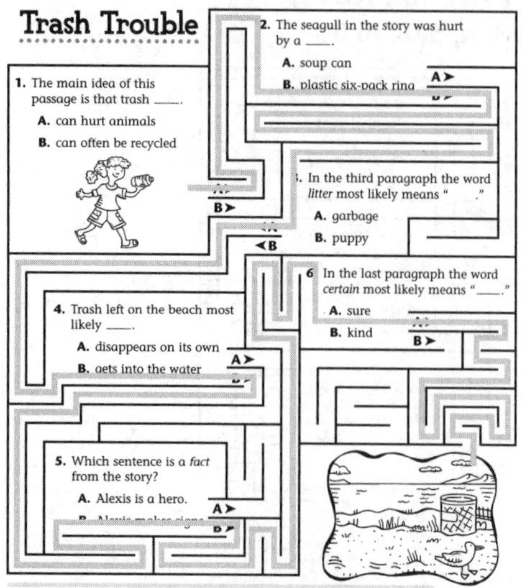

Pages 50–51 (The First Olympics)
1. A; 2. A; 3. A; 4. A; 5. A; 6. A

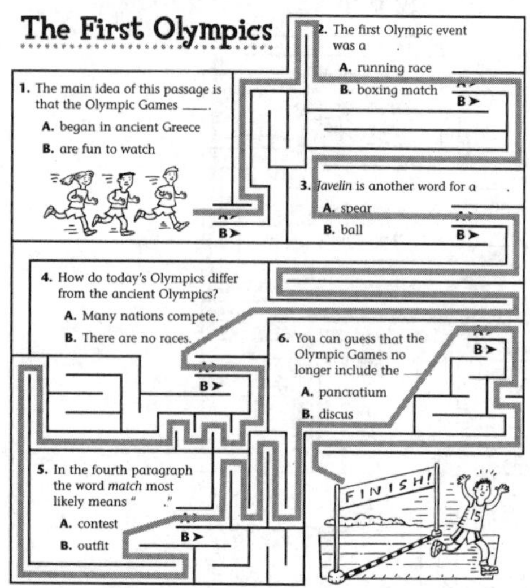

Pages 52–53 (Forest Frogs Stay Safe)
1. A; 2. A; 3. A; 4. B; 5. A; 6. A

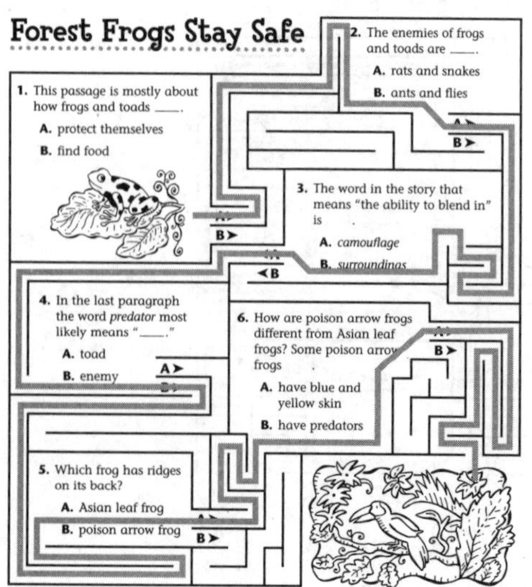

RIDDLE QUIZZES

Pages 54–55 (A School at the Zoo)
1. C; 2. H; 3. I; 4. L; 5. O; 6. S; 7. X.
Riddle: "Hi" School!

Pages 56–57 (100th Day Disaster)
1. A; 2. F; 3. G; 4. L; 5. O; 6. R; 7. W.
Riddle: A woof!

Pages 58–59 (April Fools' Day)
1. A; 2. E; 3. I; 4. L; 5. P; 6. R.
Riddle: A pear!

Pages 60–61 (The Ant and the Dove)
1. A; 2. E; 3. I; 4. M; 5. O; 6. R; 7. V; 8. Y.
Riddle: A river!

Pages 62–63 (A Dino Discovery)
1. A; 2. E; 3. F; 4. L; 5. M; 6. T; 7. W; 8. X.
Riddle: A T. Flex!

Pages 64–65 (We All Win!)
1. A; 2. C; 3. I; 4. L; 5. N; 6. P; 7. R.
Riddle: The Princi-pal!

TIC-TAC-TOE GAMES

Pages 66–67 (They Have the Beat!)
Top row, L to R: 1. A; 2. B; 3. B. Middle row, L to R: 4. B; 5. A. 6. B. Bottom row, L to R: 7. B; 8. A; 9. A

Pages 68–69 (The Friendship Box)
Top row, L to R: 1. B; 2. A; 3. B. Middle row, L to R: 4. B; 5. B. 6. A. Bottom row, L to R: 7. B; 8. A; 9. B

Pages 70–71 (Garbage in the Garden)
Top row, L to R: 1. B; 2. A; 3. B. Middle row, L to R: 4. A; 5. B. 6. B. Bottom row, L to R: 7. B; 8. A; 9. B

Pages 72–73 (Too Much TV)
Top row, L to R: 1. B; 2. B; 3. A. Middle row, L to R: 4. A; 5. B. 6. A. Bottom row, L to R: 7. B; 8. A; 9. B

Pages 74–75 (Finding Freddy)
Top row, L to R: 1. B; 2. A; 3. A. Middle row, L to R: 4. B; 5. B. 6. B. Bottom row, L to R: 7. B; 8. B; 9. A

Pages 76–77 (A Cool Inventor)
Top row, L to R: 1. A; 2. A; 3. B. Middle row, L to R: 4. A; 5. A. 6. A. Bottom row, L to R: 7. B; 8. A; 9. A

TONY SANDOVAL

WATERSNAKES

WRITTEN AND ILLUSTRATED BY

TONY SANDOVAL

Translation by Lucas Marangon

Localization, Layout, and Editing by Mike Kennedy

ISBN: 978-1-942367-75-8

Library of Congress Control Number: 2018931357

Watersnakes, published 2018 by The Lion Forge, LLC.

10 9 8 7 6 5 4 3 2 1

Chapter 1

WE COME...

...FROM FAR AWAY.

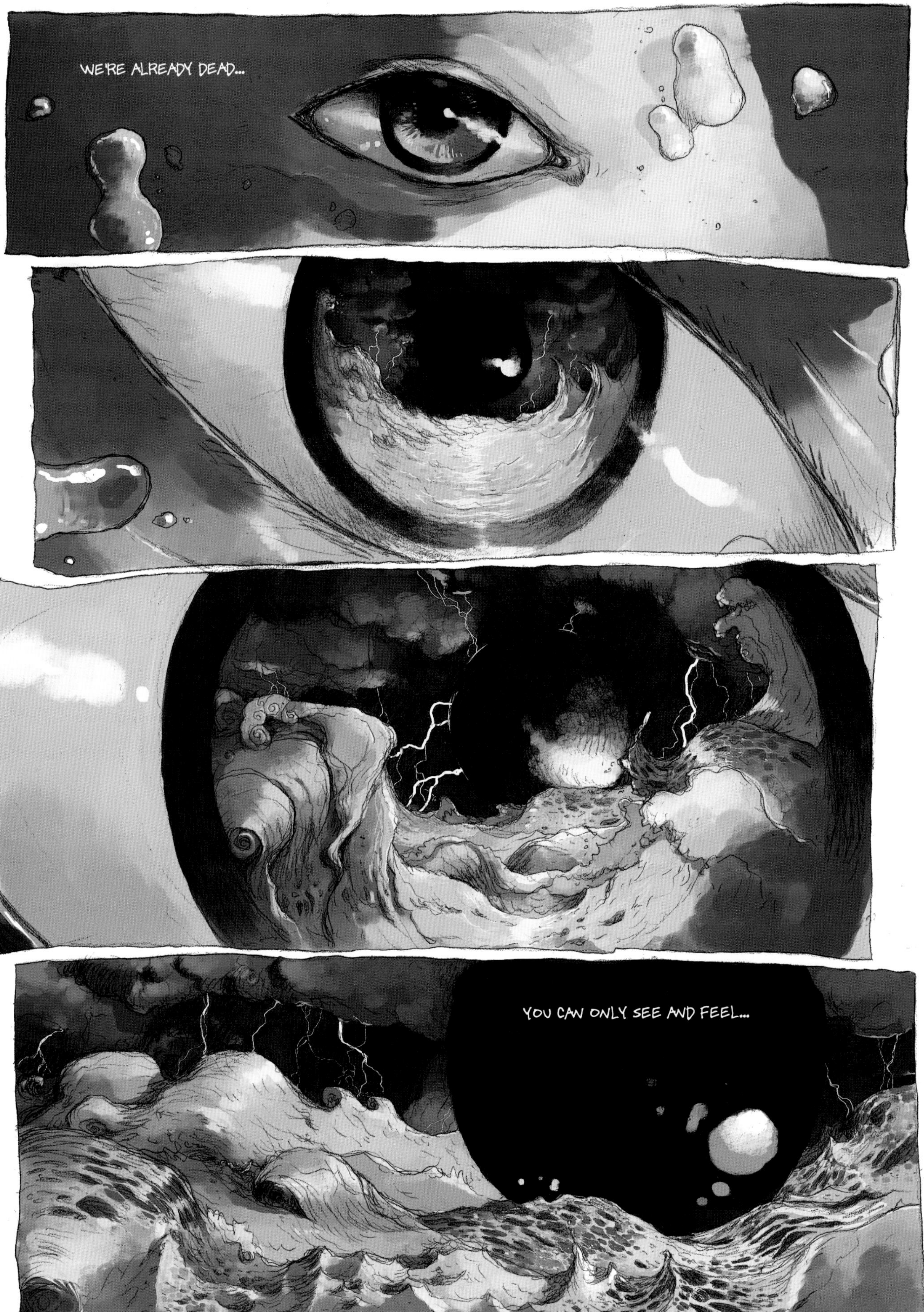
WE'RE ALREADY DEAD...
YOU CAN ONLY SEE AND FEEL...

...THE PROJECTION OF OUR ENERGY...
...LIKE THE LIGHT FROM A DEAD STAR.
THAT PROJECTION OF ENERGY PASSES THROUGH THE PRISM OF YOUR CONSCIENCE, DEFRAGMENTING ITSELF ACCORDING TO YOUR OWN INTERPRETATION.
TO EXPLODE IN A BLOSSOM...
...OF WHAT YOU HUMANS CALL MAGIC.

OOOOOOOOOOH!
A WATER SNAKE!

A WATER SNAKE?!

AHH!

WHERE IS IT?!

PFF-- IT WAS NOTHING.
HELLO, WATER SNAKE!

HEE HEE
HEE!

YOU THINK THAT'S FUNNY? SCARING STRANGERS?
OOPS! SORRY!
MY BAD -- I THOUGHT I SAW ONE, BUT IT MUST'VE BEEN YOUR HAIR...
HM.

WHO'RE YOU?

MY NAME'S AGNES. WOW, THIS IS WILD... YOU CAN SEE ME? YOU MUST BE SPECIAL!

A REAL BLACK SNAKE...

A WHAT? I'M NOTHING SPECIAL, COME ON...

I HAVEN'T SEEN YOU AROUND... I'VE NEVER SEEN ANYONE OUT HERE BEFORE, ACTUALLY!
OH, I KNOW A LOT OF SPECIAL PLACES AROUND HERE. YOU'RE PRETTY UNIQUE, THOUGH... ARE YOU FROM QUEENS?
NO, SOUTH OF MARKET.
WHOA, THAT'S FAR!
YEAH, THAT'S WHY I TAKE MY BIKE.
THERE AREN'T ANY GOOD PLACES TO SWIM AROUND THERE. BUT... WHAT MAKES YOU THINK I'M SPECIAL?
COME SEE!

I'M GONNA SHOW YOU SOMETHING AMAZING, MAYBE EVEN MAGICAL... THAT'S UP TO YOU TO DECIDE.
?
SLOWLY... BEND DOWN...

LOOK! SEE IT?
DOWN THERE...

A FOX AND HER BABIES!

AREN'T THEY BEAUTIFUL?

THEY'RE CUTE BUT HARDLY MAGICAL.

WHAT IS IT? DO YOU LIKE ME?
YOUR TEETH... CAN I TOUCH THEM?
HA!
YOU LIKE 'EM?
YEAH, THEY'RE REALLY PRETTY...
WELL, THEY'RE NOT REAL...
NOT REAL?!

THEY'RE ACTUALLY GHOSTS WHO TRAVEL THE WORLD!
HAH, YOU'RE CRAZY!
YEAH, MAYBE... AREN'T WE ALL A LITTLE CRAZY? I'LL TELL YOU THE STORY OF MY TEETH AND THEIR ADVENTURES TOMORROW IF YOU COME HUNT PICNICS WITH ME...
WHAT DO YA SAY?

WELL, IT'S A LONG RIDE HOME...
...BUT OF COURSE I'LL COME!
CRAP!
SO LATE...
I HOPE I DON'T GET IN TROUBLE...

HEY! I'M HOME!
HMF.

HEY, MILA. HOW WAS YOUR DAY?
HEY, DAD.
I WENT FOR A BIKE RIDE.

I WENT A LITTLE FAR TO GO FOR A SWIM IN THE RIVER.

BUT I MET THIS STRANGE GIRL WITH THE MOST INTERESTING TEETH!
I MEAN, SHE HAS A BEAUTIFUL SMILE...
...AND I CAN'T GET HER OUT OF MY HEAD...
DAD, YOU'RE A DENTIST. CAN I ASK YOU A QUESTION?

MILA! YOU WATCH TOO MUCH TV!
I DO NOT!

I'VE BEEN OUTSIDE ALL DAY!
I'M TIRED AND TV RELAXES ME!

SO, DAD... DO YOU HAVE TO LIKE TEETH TO DO YOUR JOB?
ER... THAT'S AN ODD QUESTION... WHY? ARE YOU THINKING ABOUT BECOMING A DENTIST?
I DUNNO. JUST WONDERING.

WE CAN TALK ABOUT IT TOMORROW. IT'S LATE.
OKAY...

DO I HAVE PRETTY TEETH, DAD?
GO TO BED, MILA.

HMPH.

THEY'RE COMING...
THEY'RE...
...COMING!
THEY'RE COMING!
AT LAST! THEY'RE COMING...

WHAT HAPPENED TO YOUR HEAD?

I WENT HUNTING FOR A CHICKEN FOR DINNER!
WOW.
ALWAYS IN A FANTASY...

LOOKS LIKE THE CHICKEN PUT UP A REAL FIGHT...
YEAH, IT GOT AWAY... BUT YOU CAME TO HEAR THE ADVENTURES OF MY TEETH, DIDN'T YOU?
YES! SPILL!

SOMETIMES, WHEN I'M ALONE AT NIGHT, THEY ASK ME TO LET THEM GO...

I FEEL WEIRD WITHOUT THEM, SO I SLIDE MY TONGUE OVER THE HOLES...
MEANWHILE, THEY'RE OFF EXPLORING THE UNIVERSE, ACROSS SPACE AND TIME...
WHEN THEY COME BACK, THEY TELL ME ABOUT ALL THE WONDERFUL THINGS THEY SAW...
BLAH BLAH BLAH...
REALLY? HUH...
LOOK! A PICNIC!

LET'S GO! MASKS ON!

FOLLOW ME! WE'RE ANIMALS NOW, GOT IT?
I'M A FOX AND YOU'RE A WATER SNAKE WITH A RABBIT MASK!
HEH HEH!

RAAAARHHH!
ARGH!

HAHAHAHHH!
DID YOU LIKE THAT? IT'S FUN, RIGHT?!
YES! I MEAN, I WAS SCARED AT FIRST, BUT... THEN I LOVED IT! SO EASY!
LET'S GO HIDE OUR LOOT!
I KNEW DEEP DOWN YOU WERE A LITTLE CRIMINAL...
HOW DO I LOOK?
TAKE OFF THE MASK. I WANNA SEE YOUR SMILE...
WHY? ARE YOU INTO GIRLS?
WE HAVE POWERS!

I DON'T KNOW.
I... I NEVER THOUGHT ABOUT IT. I SWEAR.
IT'S COOL, I BELIEVE YOU.
AND I DON'T CARE!

BUT...
YOU DON'T BITE... DO YOU, WATERSNAKE?

WHAT'S THAT SUPPOSED TO MEAN?!
I'M JUST TEASING! YOU LIKE WHEN I TEASE YOU!
SHIT, SHE'S RIGHT...
NO I DON'T!
HA HA HA!
OH, YOU'RE SO CUTE WHEN YOU'RE MAD!
I THINK YOU'RE THE ONE WHO'S INTO GIRLS!
NOPE, I'VE GOT A BOYFRIEND!
WH...? REALLY?

DON'T MAKE SUCH A SAD FACE. IT'S JUST A FLING.

WHATEVER. YOU CAN DO WHAT YOU WANT.

OF COURSE I CAN!
HA HA!

WAIT... DO YOU FEEL SOMETHING STRANGE...?

DID THE PICNIC PEOPLE FOLLOW US?!
NO NO... NOT THAT. SOMETHING ELSE... SOMETHING SUPERNATURAL...

Y-YEAH... I THINK I FEEL IT, TOO...

ROAAR!
AAH!
YOU ASSHOLE!
HA HA HA!
LET'S JUST GO...

HO HO HO... OH MAN, YOUR FACE...

LOOKS LIKE A STORM IS BREWING...
A FAT ONE, TOO...
LET'S GO TO MY PLACE. IT'S NOT FAR.
OKAY, LET'S HURRY! THIS SNAKE HATES WATER!
SOON...
OH NO!
WOOF! WE MADE IT!
HAHAHA! YEAH, JUST BARELY!
COME ON!
ARE YOU COMING?!

UH, HI!

WEIRDO...

IS THAT KID DOWNSTAIRS YOUR BROTHER?
YEP. COME HERE...

I'LL READ YOU A STORY WHILE WE WAIT FOR THE RAIN TO STOP.
OKAY...

WHAT BOOK?
YOU'LL SEE!

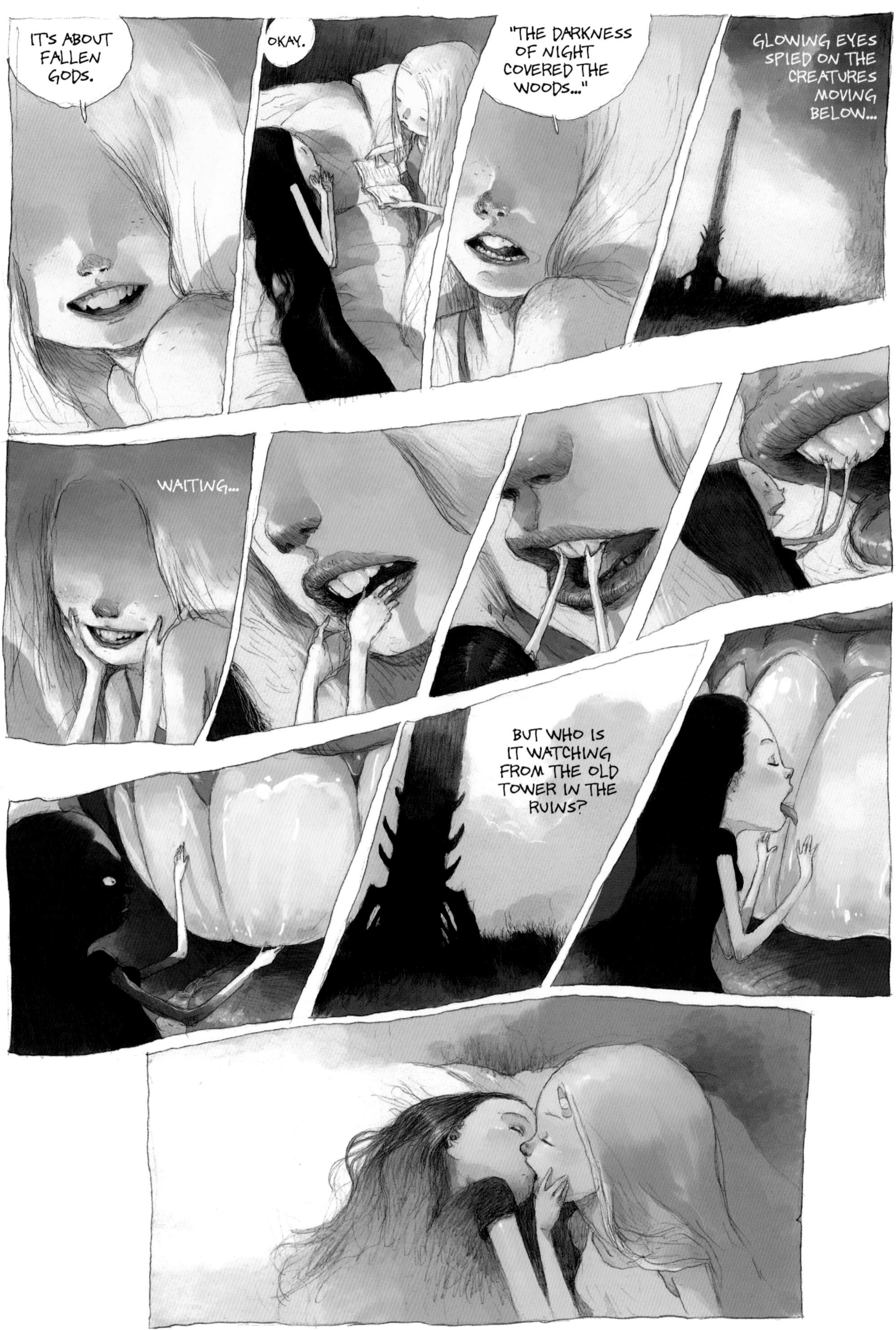
IT'S ABOUT FALLEN GODS.
OKAY.
"THE DARKNESS OF NIGHT COVERED THE WOODS..."
GLOWING EYES SPIED ON THE CREATURES MOVING BELOW...
WAITING...
BUT WHO IS IT WATCHING FROM THE OLD TOWER IN THE RUINS?

OH GOD!
WH--
UGH, ARE YOU CRAZY?!
NO, YOU STARTED IT!
THAT WAS... SURREAL!
TOTALLY!

OOF, I FEEL WEIRD...

OW! IT HURTS...
WAS IT THE KISS? I'M SORRY!

DON'T BE A DUMMY! HOW'S A KISS SUPPOSED TO HURT...?

OH MY GOD!

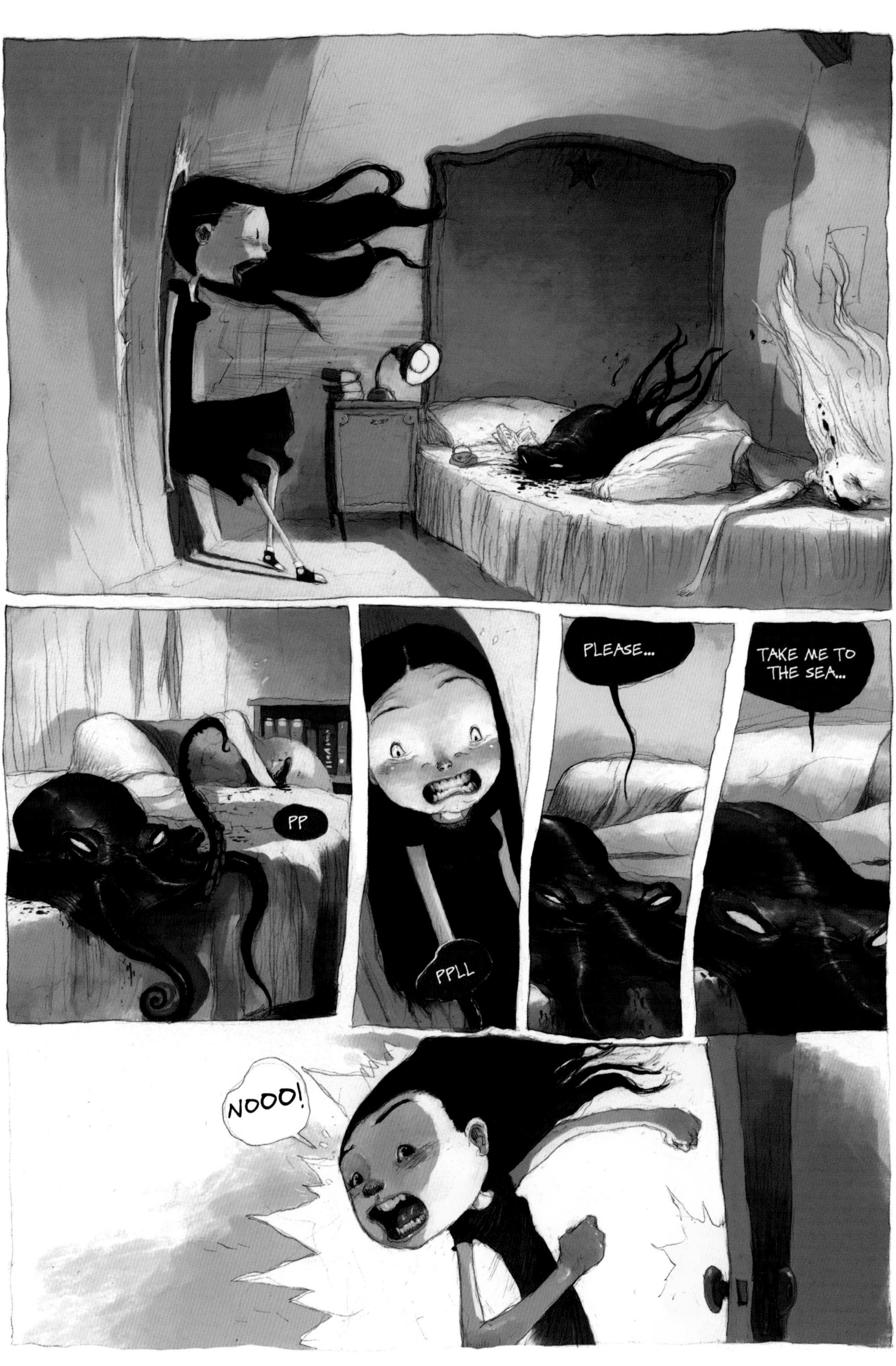

PP
PPLL
PLEASE...
TAKE ME TO THE SEA...
NOOO!

TAP!
TAP!

Chapter 2

THE SUMMER GREW OLD...

I COULD FEEL ITS LAST BREATH EVERYWHERE...

SOME BROWN STAINS HERE, SOME YELLOW ONES THERE...

IT HAD GROWN TIRED OF KEEPING THINGS WARM AND COLORFUL...

IT WAS ALONE... LIKE ME.

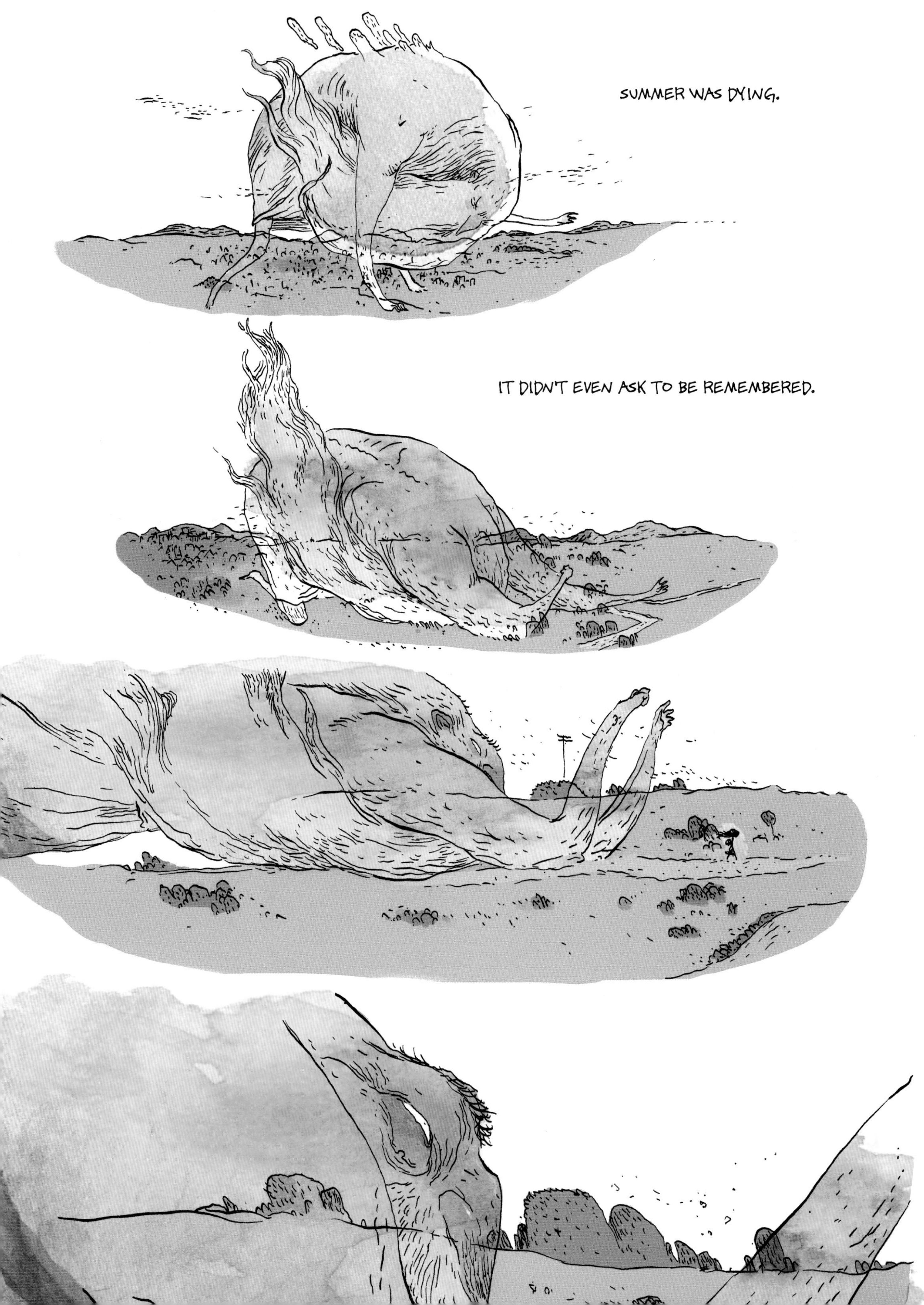
SUMMER WAS DYING.
IT DIDN'T EVEN ASK TO BE REMEMBERED.

NOT EVEN AS A DYING WISH.

5

MY BIKE!

YOU LEFT YOUR PURSE, TOO. THAT'S HOW I FINALLY FOUND YOU.

THANK YOU! THAT WAS NICE OF YOU TO COME ALL THE WAY HERE!

LOOK, I DUNNO WHAT HAPPENED THE OTHER DAY...

...BUT AGNES IS A GOOD GIRL.

I KNOW.

SO...

...I JUST WANTED YOU TO HAVE YOUR STUFF BACK.

LATER.

SO I GUESS SHE DOESN'T WANT TO SEE ME AGAIN...

WELL, THAT CHANGES EVERYTHING.

WAIT!

ARE YOU THIRSTY? I'LL BUY YOU A DRINK... AS A THANK-YOU...

...OKAY.

WHAT'S YOUR NAME?
JULIEN.

IS AGNES OKAY?
I GUESS.

IS SHE MAD AT ME?

I DUNNO.

HOW COME?

WELL, IT'S COMPLICATED...
I LEFT HER ALONE WITH THAT CREATURE...
YOU KNOW? THE OCTOPUS THAT... UM...
NO.
YOU DON'T KNOW ANYTHING ABOUT AGNES.
HUH?
AGNES DIED ELEVEN YEARS AGO.
SHUT UP.

THAT'S IMPOSSIBLE.

UNLESS... DID SHE PUT YOU UP TO THIS?

THAT'S HER KIND OF JOKE!

NO JOKE.

MOM TOLD ME SHE DIED OF POISONING WHEN SHE WAS FIVE.

BUT I CAN HEAR HER WHEN SHE TALKS.

I THINK SHE LIKES THE PAPER MASKS I MAKE.
I KNOW SHE STILL USES HER BEDROOM.

BUT MOM TOLD ME NOT TO TALK ABOUT HER.

I KNOW THIS SOUNDS REALLY SAD.

I SHOULD GO. YOU'RE LUCKY YOU CAN SEE HER.

THANKS FOR THE SODA.

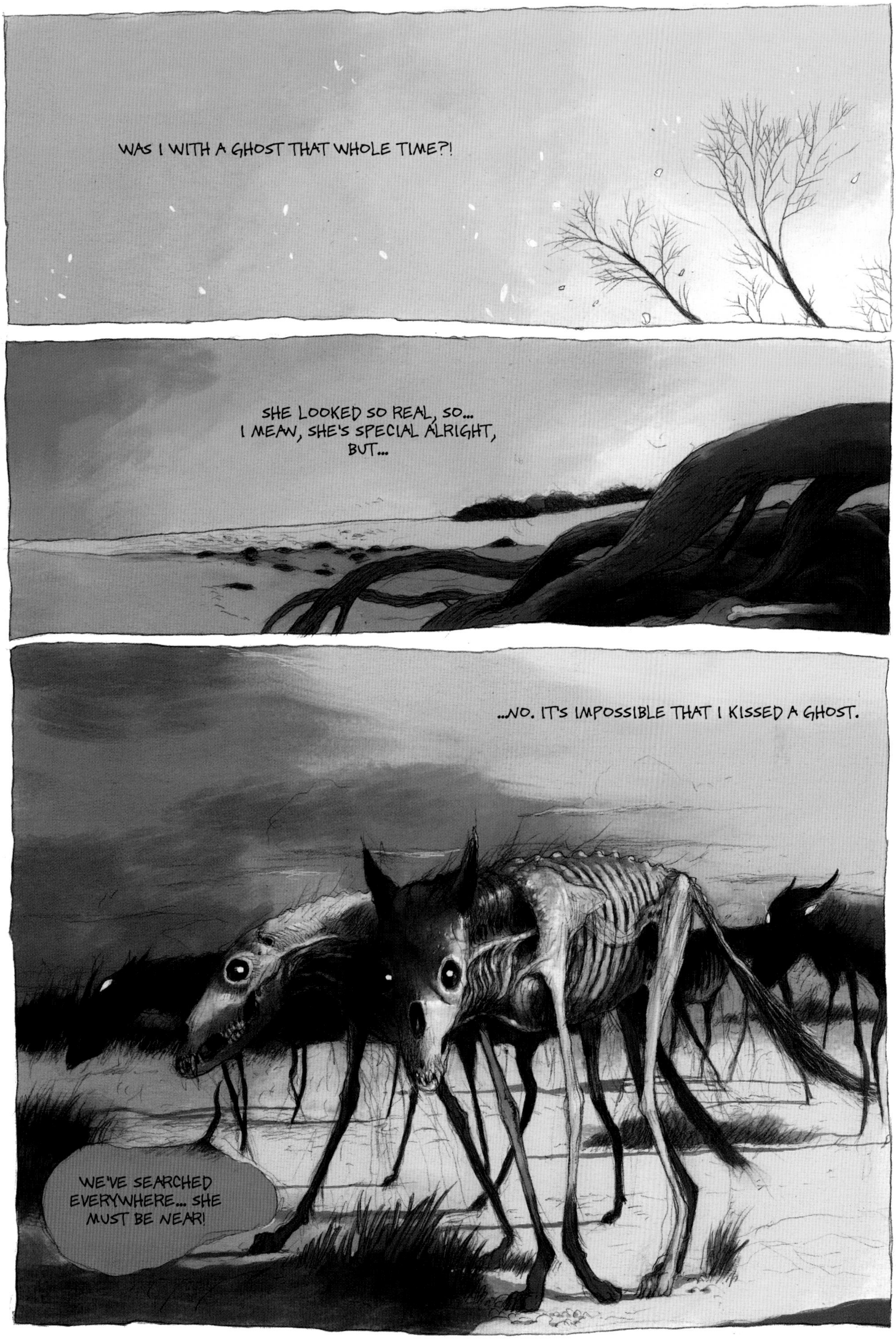

...NO. IT'S IMPOSSIBLE THAT I KISSED A GHOST.

WE'VE SEARCHED EVERYWHERE... SHE MUST BE NEAR!

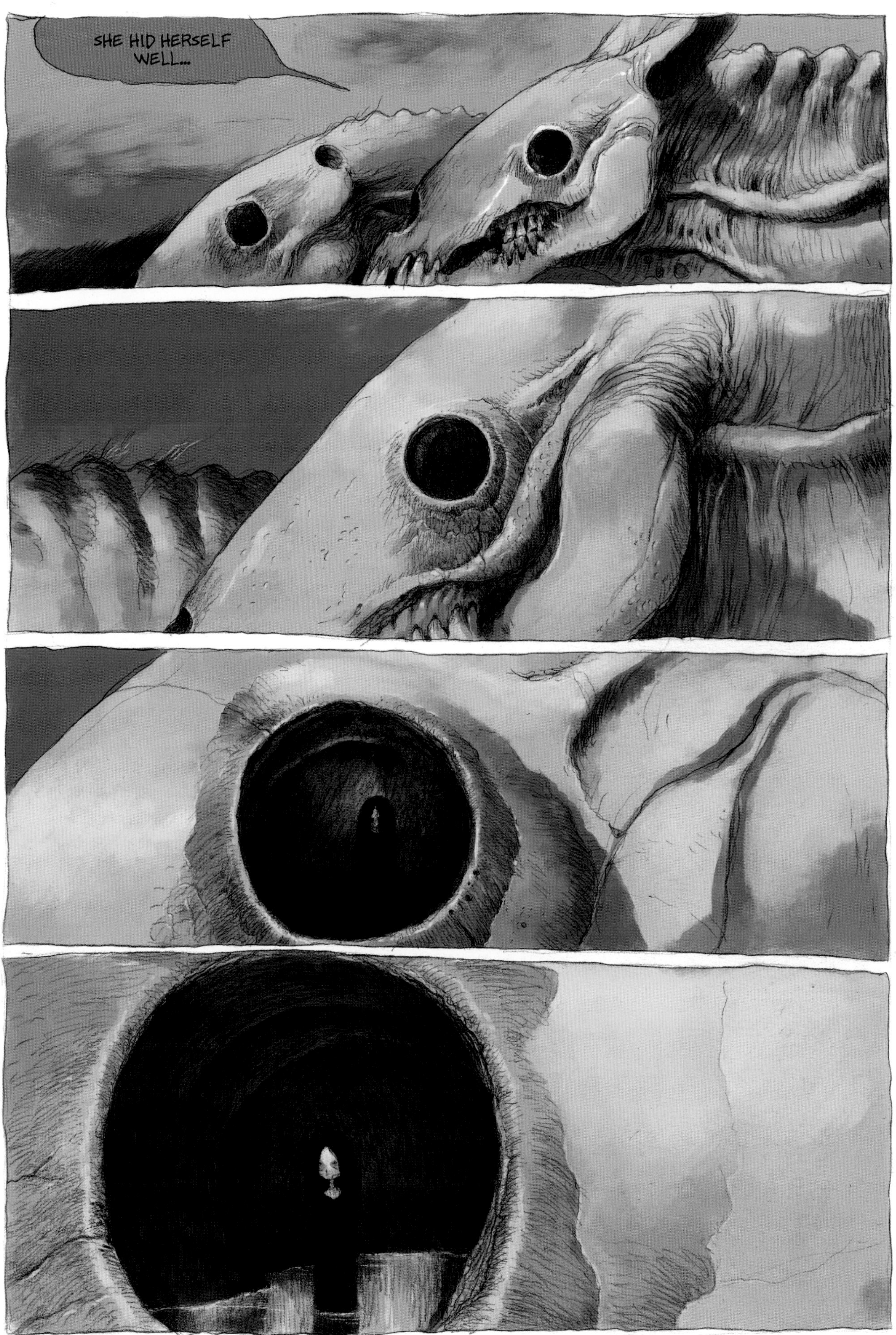
SHE HID HERSELF WELL...

THEY'RE COMING.

WHO?
THEY'RE COMING...
...TO KILL HIM!
KILL WHO?!
WHO ARE YOU?! SHOW YOURSELF!

THEY'RE COMING TO KILL THE KING.

YOU!
YOU'RE... ONE OF AGNES'S... TEETH?

KOF
KOF

Chapter 3

I CAN'T STOP THINKING
ABOUT HER...

...AND HER
AMAZING TEETH.

I WISH THEY WERE MINE, BUT
THE VERY IDEA IS STUPID.

IT'S BEEN A WHILE...
I'D REALLY LIKE TO
SEE HER AGAIN...

...EVEN FROM
A DISTANCE.

...WHERE'D SHE GO?!
THERE!
UFF...
...HOW CAN SHE WALK SO FAST?!
WOO!

SHE WENT INTO TOWN! IT'S GONNA BE HARD TO FOLLOW HER THERE...

I'VE GOTTA CATCH UP!

WOW, SHE'S SHOP-LIFTING LIKE CRAZY...!
GUESS THAT SHOULDN'T SURPRISE ME...

BUT NO ONE SEES HER...

DAMN IT! WHERE'D SHE GO?!

ARGH!
SHE'S GONE!

AS IF...

...SHE WAS A...
FES

...GHOST.

OH!

WHAT A SURPRISE! WHAT ARE YOU DOING HERE?
ER... NOTHING.

Y'KNOW, I'M MAD AT YOU...
...BUT GLAD TO SEE YOU, TOO.
OH.
REALLY?
ACTUALLY, I'M REALLY HAPPY TO SEE YOU.
OH!

Y'KNOW...

...YOUR BROTHER CAME BY MY HOUSE THE OTHER DAY...
HE DID?

HE BROUGHT MY BIKE BACK AND TOLD ME A WEIRD STORY ABOUT YOU.

HE SAYS YOU'RE A GHOST!
CRAZY, HUH?

HONESTLY...? I'VE GOT SOMETHING TO TELL YOU. FOLLOW ME...

IS THIS ANOTHER ONE OF YOUR JOKES?

NO, BUT BEFORE WE GO, I HAVE A QUESTION...
WHAT'S YOUR NAME?

I WAS FIVE YEARS OLD WHEN I FIRST SAW THE OCTOPUS.
HEY, THERE!
ARE YOU HURT?
YOU'RE SO CUTE!

AGNES! COME ON!
OH NO!
MOM WON'T LET ME KEEP YOU...
AGNES!
GULP!
BLEAGH! TASTES BAD!
THEN I GOT SICK.
I LOST ALL MY BABY TEETH IN ONE NIGHT.
BUT THE NEXT DAY, I FELT BETTER.

BUT SOMETHING WAS WRONG.

SOB
MOM! MOMMA! MOM! MOMMY! MOM! MOM!
MY PARENTS COULDN'T SEE OR HEAR ME...

THE HOUSE WAS FILLED WITH POLICEMEN...
HEY! I'M HERE!

...AND ETERNAL SADNESS.

THOSE WERE DAYS OF INFINITE CRUELTY.
I CAME TO THE CONCLUSION THAT I NO LONGER EXISTED, BUT I STILL GOT HUNGRY, COLD, AND TIRED...
WHO TOOK MY SANDWICH?
LUCKILY I COULD ALREADY READ, SO I'VE BEEN ABLE TO ENTERTAIN MYSELF.
MY LITTLE BROTHER COULD HEAR ME, BUT MY MOM DIDN'T BELIEVE HIM.
SO I SPENT MY TIME SPOOKING THE OTHER KIDS IN THE NEIGHBORHOOD BY WHISPERING WICKED THINGS IN THEIR EARS...
BUT YOU... YOU'RE SPECIAL!
BECAUSE YOU CAN SEE ME!

I THINK YOU'RE MAGICAL.

I'M NOT THAT SPECIAL, REALLY.
I'M BORING AND ORDINARY...

ESPECIALLY COMPARED TO YOUR UNBELIEVABLE STORY!

YOU SAW THE OCTOPUS, RIGHT?
YEAH... TRUE...

EGH, SO GROSS...

I ACTUALLY LEARNED A LOT SINCE I THREW HIM UP.

LIKE, I HAVE TO FREE HIM TONIGHT!

BIG THINGS ARE ABOUT TO HAPPEN TONIGHT...
WILL YOU GO WITH ME?

I DUNNO...

PLEASE, I NEED YOUR HELP FOR THE LIBERATION RITUAL...

IS IT SOME KIND OF PAGAN OR SATANIC THING?
BOTH!
WOW.
WHERE DO WE DO IT?
I HID THE OCTOPUS IN SOME RUINS NO ONE GOES TO.
ARE WE GOING TO SACRIFICE THE OCTOPUS?
WHAT? NO!

WEIRD.

WEIRD IS THE NEW NORMAL, MILA.

HERE WE ARE! WHAT DO YOU THINK?

WHOA.

I HAD NO IDEA A PLACE LIKE THIS COULD EXIST...
IT'S A SECRET.
PEOPLE ARE AFRAID TO COME HERE. THEY DON'T EVEN TALK ABOUT IT.

WHY?
'CUZ IT'S HAUNTED!

WHERE'S THE OCTOPUS?

THERE, IN THE FOUNTAIN.

IT'S AN OLD GARDEN WITH ACCESS TO THE BEACH.
THE STAIRS...

...I FEEL LIKE I'VE SEEN THEM BEFORE... STRANGE...

GO GET SOME FIREWOOD FOR THE CEREMONY.

I'LL MAKE THE CIRCLE.

UGH, THIS PLACE GIVES ME THE CREEPS... I BET ALL KINDS OF BAD STUFF HAPPENED HERE...

WAIT... NOW I REMEMBER! I'VE SEEN THIS PLACE IN MY DREAMS...!

TOO WEIRD!
JUST LIKE ALL THOSE DOGS...

AGNES?

THE CIRCLE'S DONE!

NOW WE JUST HAVE TO FALL ASLEEP!

FALL ASLEEP?! WITH THOSE DOGS OUT THERE? CAN'T YOU FEEL THEM?

DON'T BE AFRAID. THE CIRCLE WILL PROTECT US.
WHAT?!

THE OCTOPUS SAYS WE HAVE TO SLEEP TO REACH A STATE OF LIBERATION.
WHAT DOES THAT MEAN?!

FINE. WHATEVER! LET'S GO TO SLEEP!

WAIT, PUT ON YOUR RITUAL CAPE FIRST...

HOW AM I SUPPOSED TO FALL ASLEEP?!

HA HA. "JUST LIE DOWN."
YOU'RE SO ANNOYING.

ZZZZ
ALREADY? WOW!

I CAN HEAR THE ENGINES AND WHEELS OF EVERY CAR ON THE FREEWAY IN THE DISTANCE. I CAN HEAR EVERY WAVE THAT BREAKS AGAINST THE SHORE...

I CAN HEAR THE SECRET STREAMS FULL OF WATER SNAKES...
I CAN HEAR THE CHILDREN OF THE STORM CALLING FOR THEIR KING.

BUT TONIGHT, PACKS OF DEAD WOLVES
WILL HUNT US DOWN...

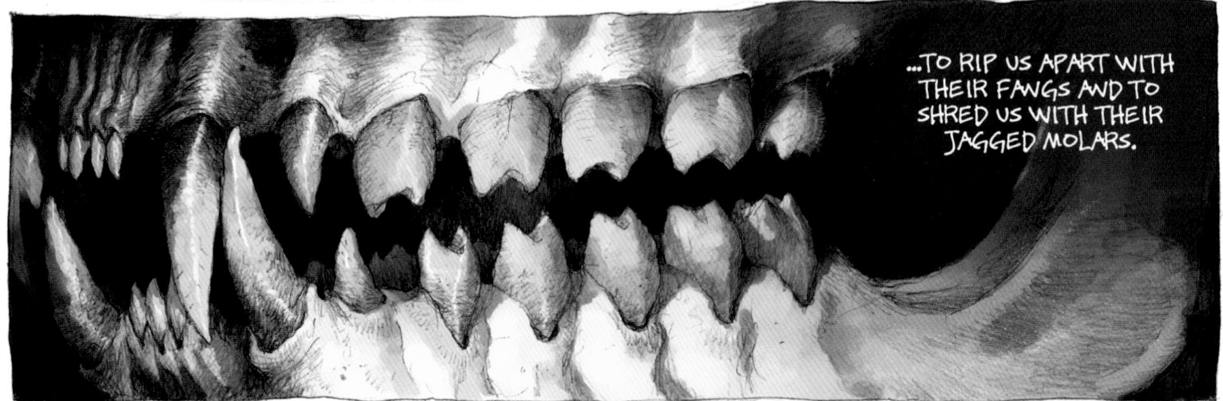
...TO RIP US APART WITH THEIR FANGS AND TO SHRED US WITH THEIR JAGGED MOLARS.

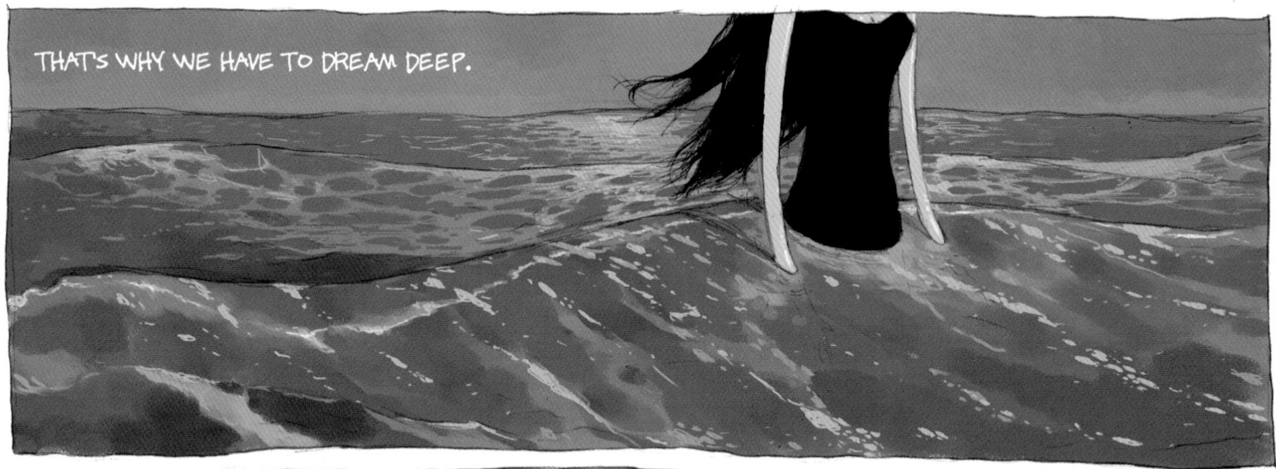
THAT'S WHY WE HAVE TO DREAM DEEP.

SO DEEP THEY CAN'T REACH US.

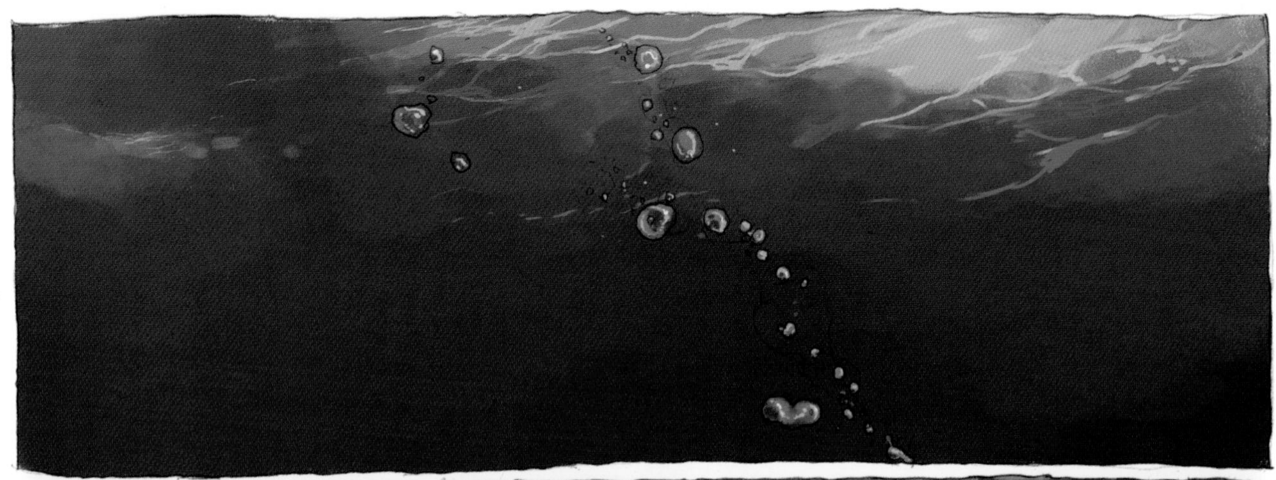

THEY'RE HERE!

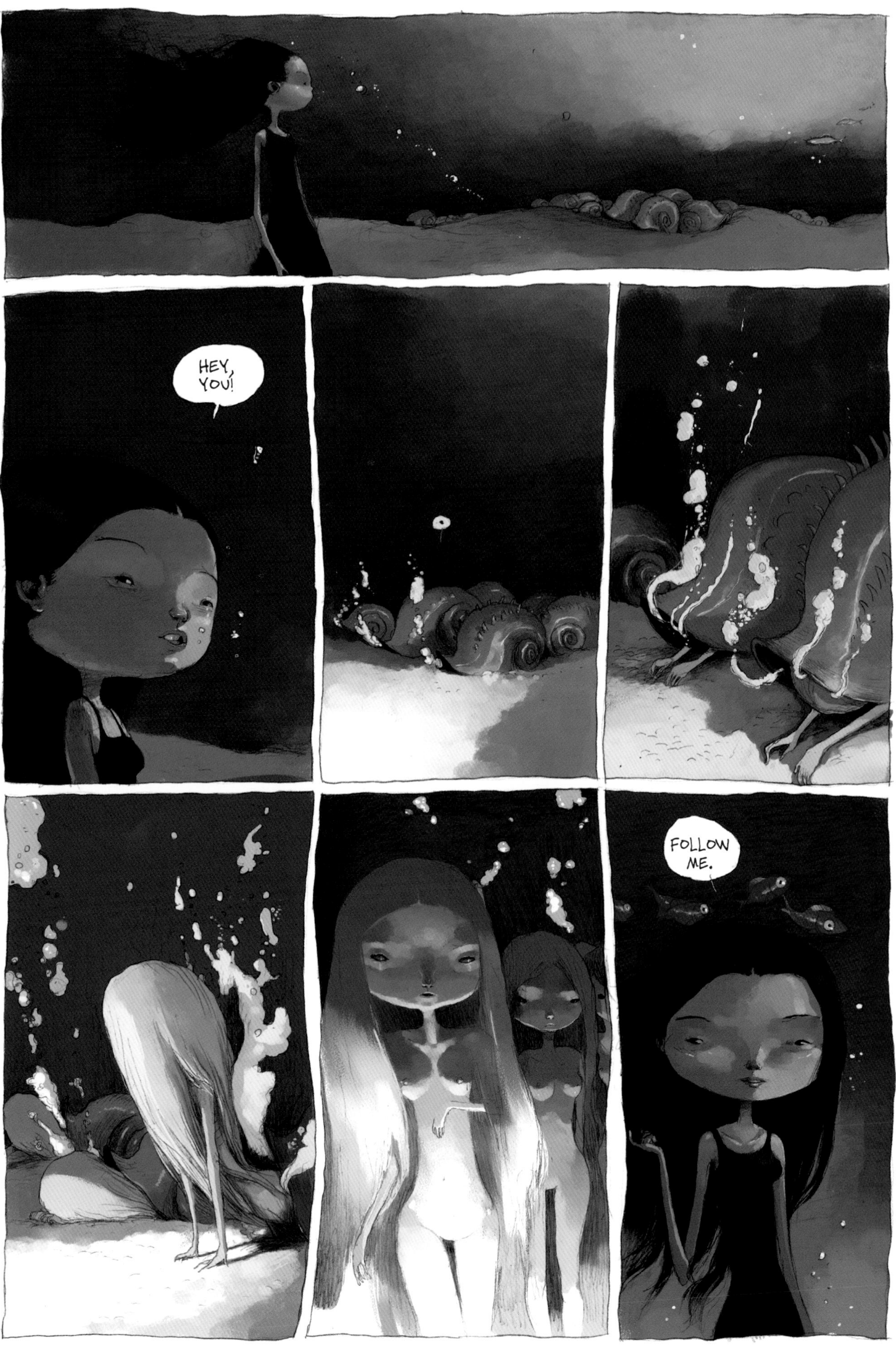
HEY, YOU!
FOLLOW ME.

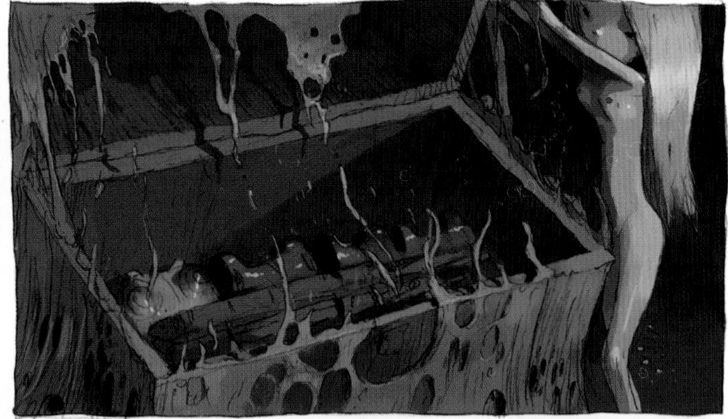

AH!

I CAN SEE ALL THE TEETH NOW!
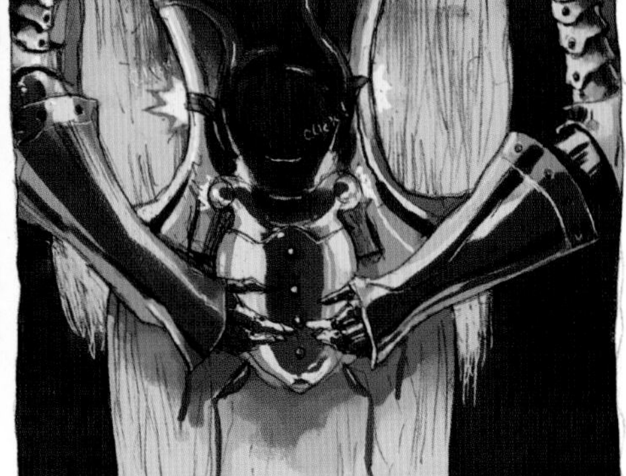

WE'RE READY FOR BATTLE.

AH HAH!

WHO ARE THEY?
SERVANTS?

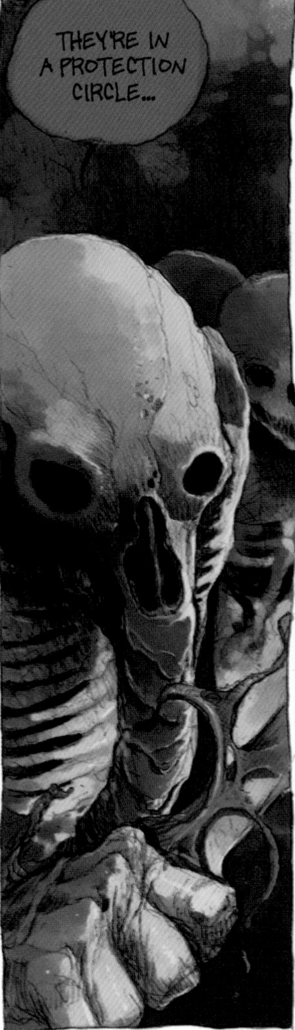
THEY'RE IN A PROTECTION CIRCLE...

INTERESTING... ONE OF THE SERVANTS ACTS AS AN ANTENNA. I DON'T LIKE THAT.
SOMETHING STRANGE IS GOING ON...

DESTROY THAT STUPID CIRCLE!
COME OUT OF THERE!
WHA--?
LOOK OUT!

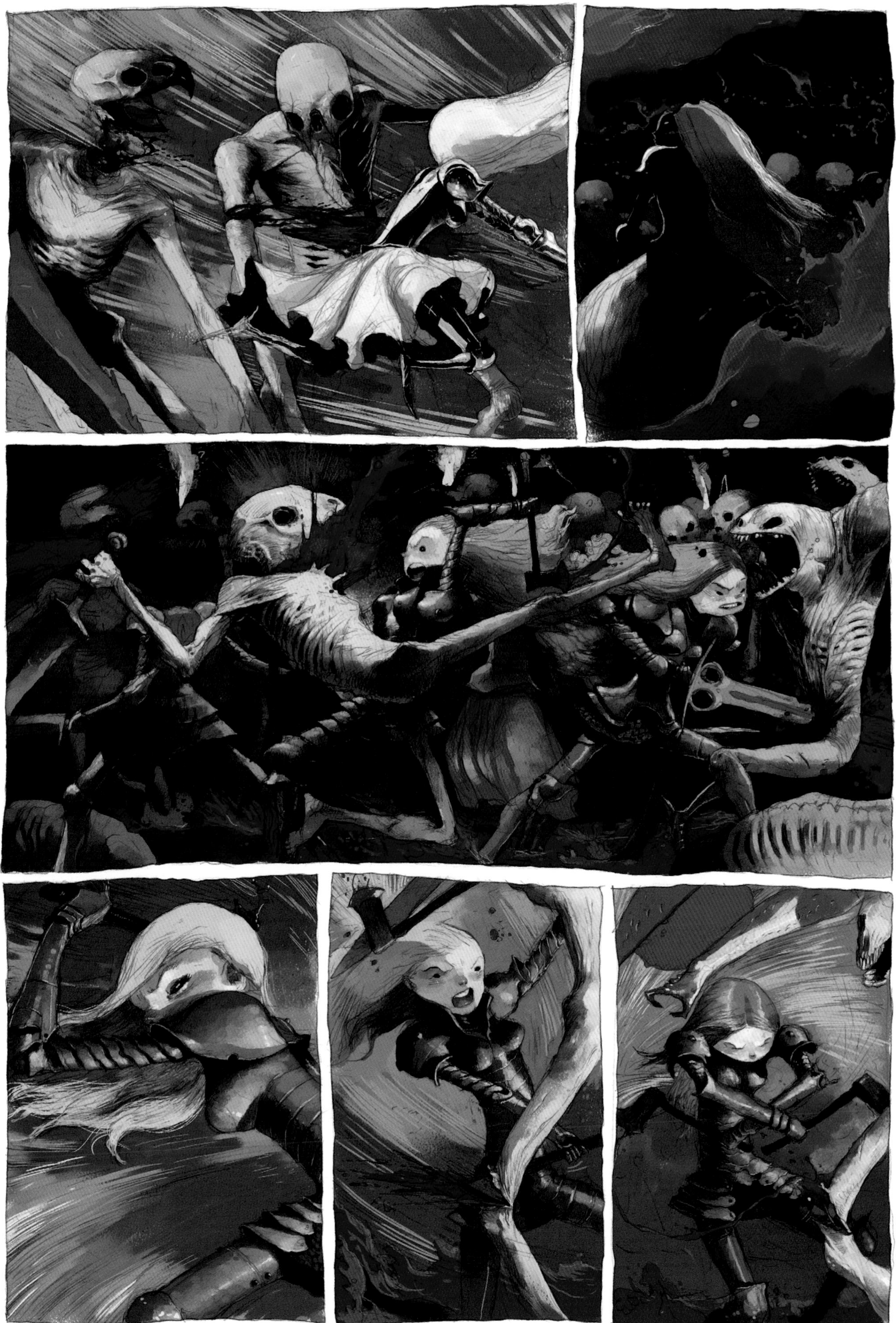

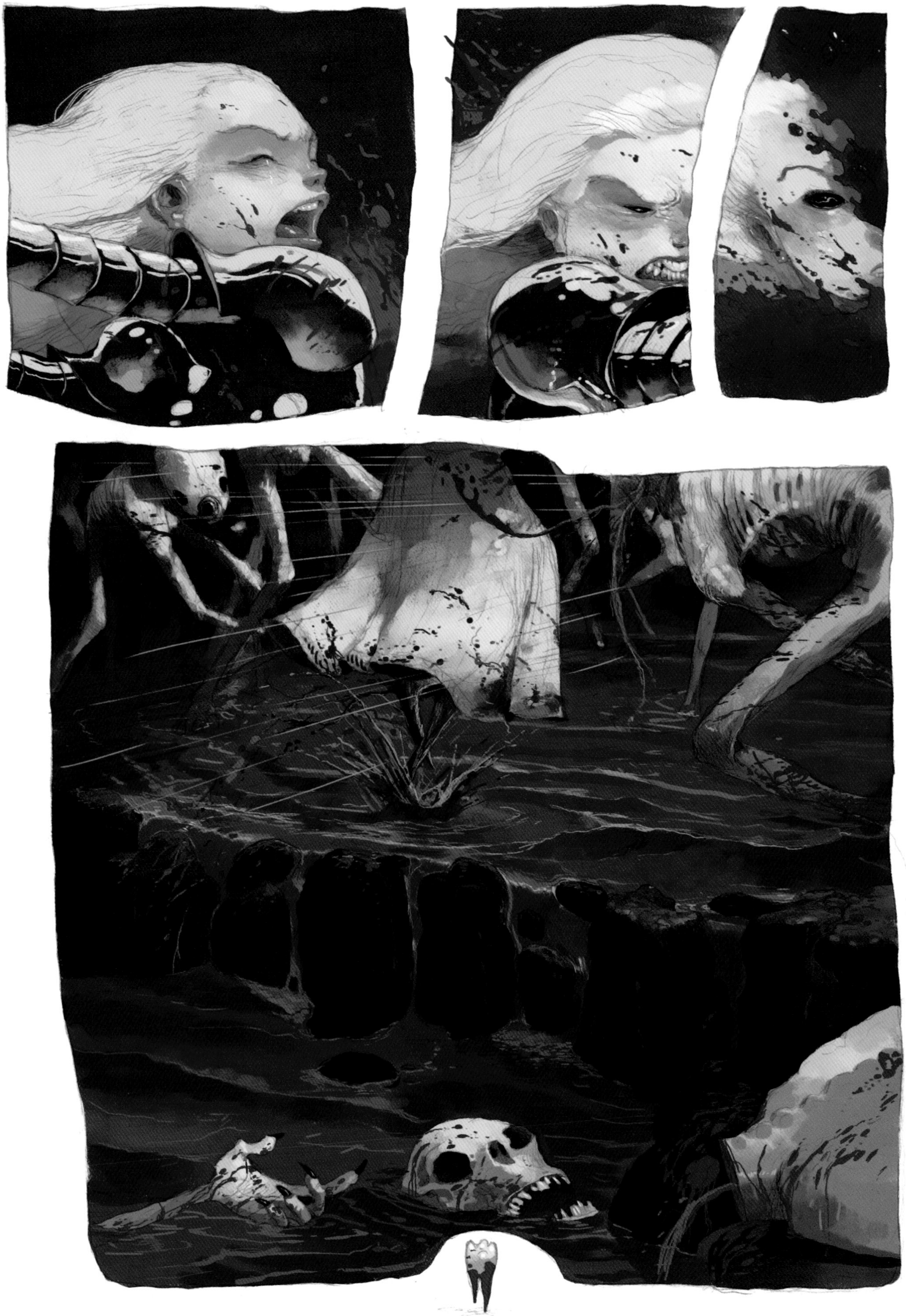

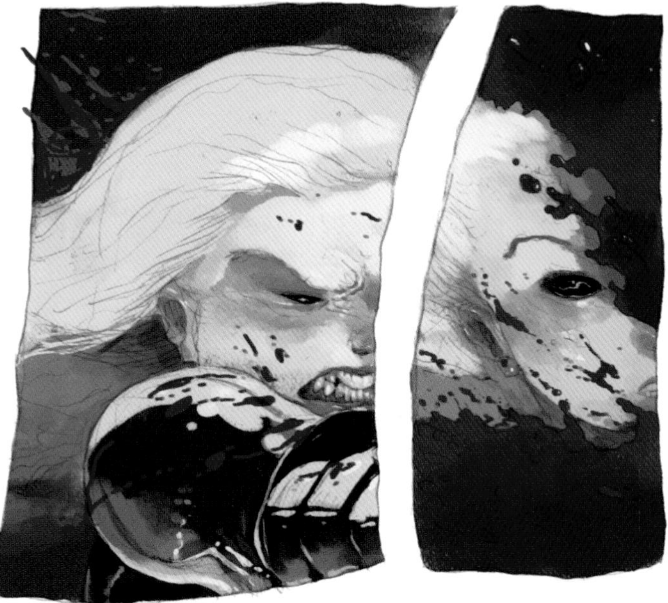

SO MUCH BLOOD...
YOU! OVER HERE!
TAKE ME TO THE SEA!
WHY DO YOU KEEP ASKING THAT?!
THIS WOULDN'T HAVE HAPPENED IF YOU DID IT WHEN I FIRST ASKED!
BUT... THAT'S ME!

WOW... I'M PRETTY WHEN I SLEEP...
AND...
OH MY GOD!
AGNES!
WHAT'S--
OH NO!
HER TEETH!
SHE'S LOSING THEM! TH-THAT MEANS...
...THEY CAN BE MINE!
MINE!
MINE!
I'VE WANTED THEM SINCE THE FIRST TIME I SAW THEM...
WHAT DO I DO?!
I...
...I GOTTA GET OUT OF HERE!
HEY!
WHERE ARE YOU GOING?!

COWARD!
YEAH, YEAH, KEEP TALKING!

I...

...I'VE BEEN AN IDIOT!

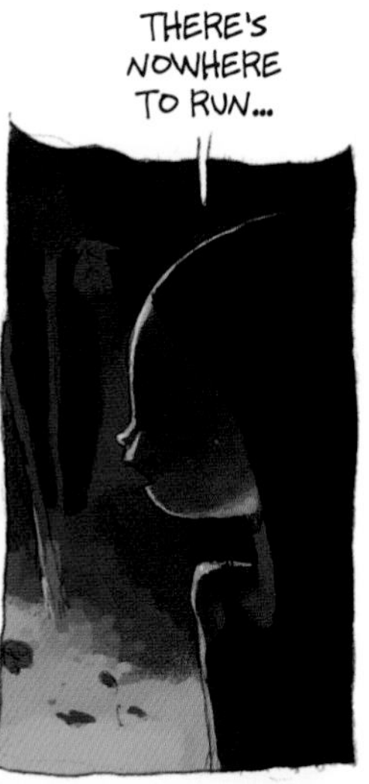
THERE'S NOWHERE TO RUN...

I HAVE TO GO BACK TO MY BODY...
I CAN'T ABANDON AGNES AGAIN.

...BUT I'M SO SCARED!
THIS IS A TOTAL NIGHTMARE!
I SHOULDN'T BE DREAMING THIS!
THERE YOU ARE. I WAS WAITING FOR YOU.
ME?
THERE'S TOO MANY OF THEM. WE CAN'T HOLD OUT MUCH LONGER.
TAKE THE SACRED OCTOPUS AND FOLLOW ME.
EUGH... DO I HAVE TO... TOUCH IT?
YES! PICK IT UP!

O-OKAY... ONE SECOND...

I HAVE TO HIDE THESE TEETH IN A SAFE PLACE... LIKE MY POCKET!

SO... WHY DO I HAVE TO CARRY IT? WHY CAN'T YOU?

BECAUSE THIS IS YOUR DREAM.

AHHH, RIGHT.

BLEAGH!

NOW WHAT?

TO THE STAIRCASE!
BYE, GIRLS! SEE YOU SOON!

STRANGE... I DON'T MIND CARRYING THIS THING ANYMORE...

IN FACT, I THINK I CAN FEEL HIS EMOTIONS!

STAY FOCUSED!
WE HAVE TO GET HIM ALL THE WAY TO THE BEACH!

THIS UNDERGROUND GROTTO IS A SHORTCUT.

HOPEFULLY THE WAY IS CLEAR...

SO WHY IS THIS OCTOPUS SO IMPORTANT?
BECAUSE HE'S OUR KING.

WH... REALY?! I MEAN... SURE, WHY NOT?

HE WAS BETRAYED BY HIS FAMILY DURING THE LONG WAR BETWEEN THE EARTH AND SEA... THEY IMPRISONED HIM FOR THOUSANDS OF YEARS.

ONE DAY, HE MANAGED TO ESCAPE, BUT HE WAS TOO WEAK.

WE COULDN'T HELP HIM, SO HE ENDED UP STRANDED ON THE BEACH WHERE HE TOOK THE FORM OF AN OCTOPUS.

BUT HOW DO WE FIT INTO THIS STORY?
YOUR FRIEND SWALLOWED THE KING WHEN HE WAS IN HIS MOST FRAGILE FORM...

...IMPRISONED BEHIND HER TEETH UNTIL SHE MET YOU.
SO... AGNES WON'T BE A GHOST ANYMORE?

YOUR FRIEND IS HALF-REAL AND HALF-DREAM.
BUT IF OUR KING DOESN'T RETURN TO THE SEA...

...SHE'LL REMAIN ONE OF YOUR DREAMS FOREVER.

OH...

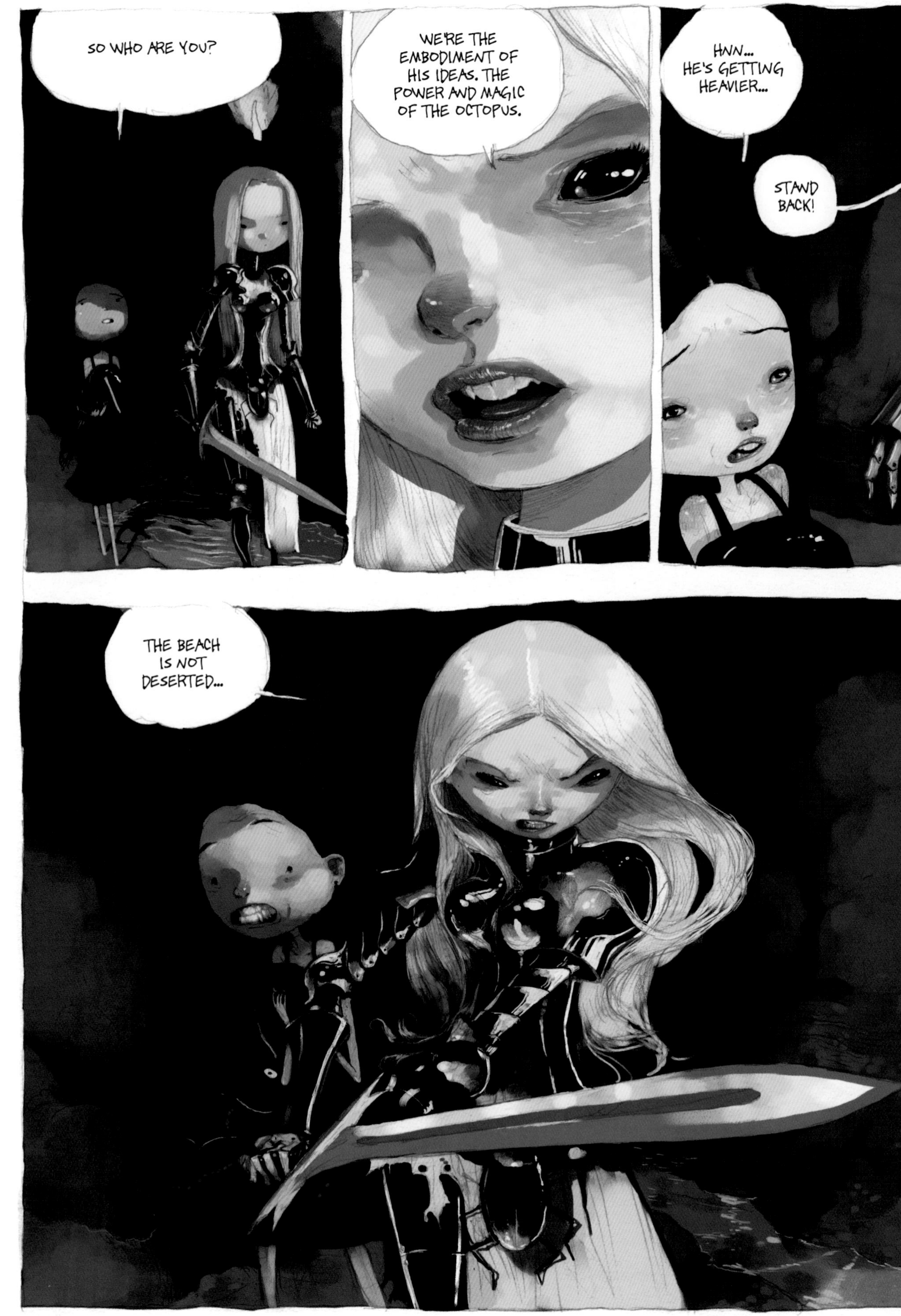

THE BEACH IS NOT DESERTED...

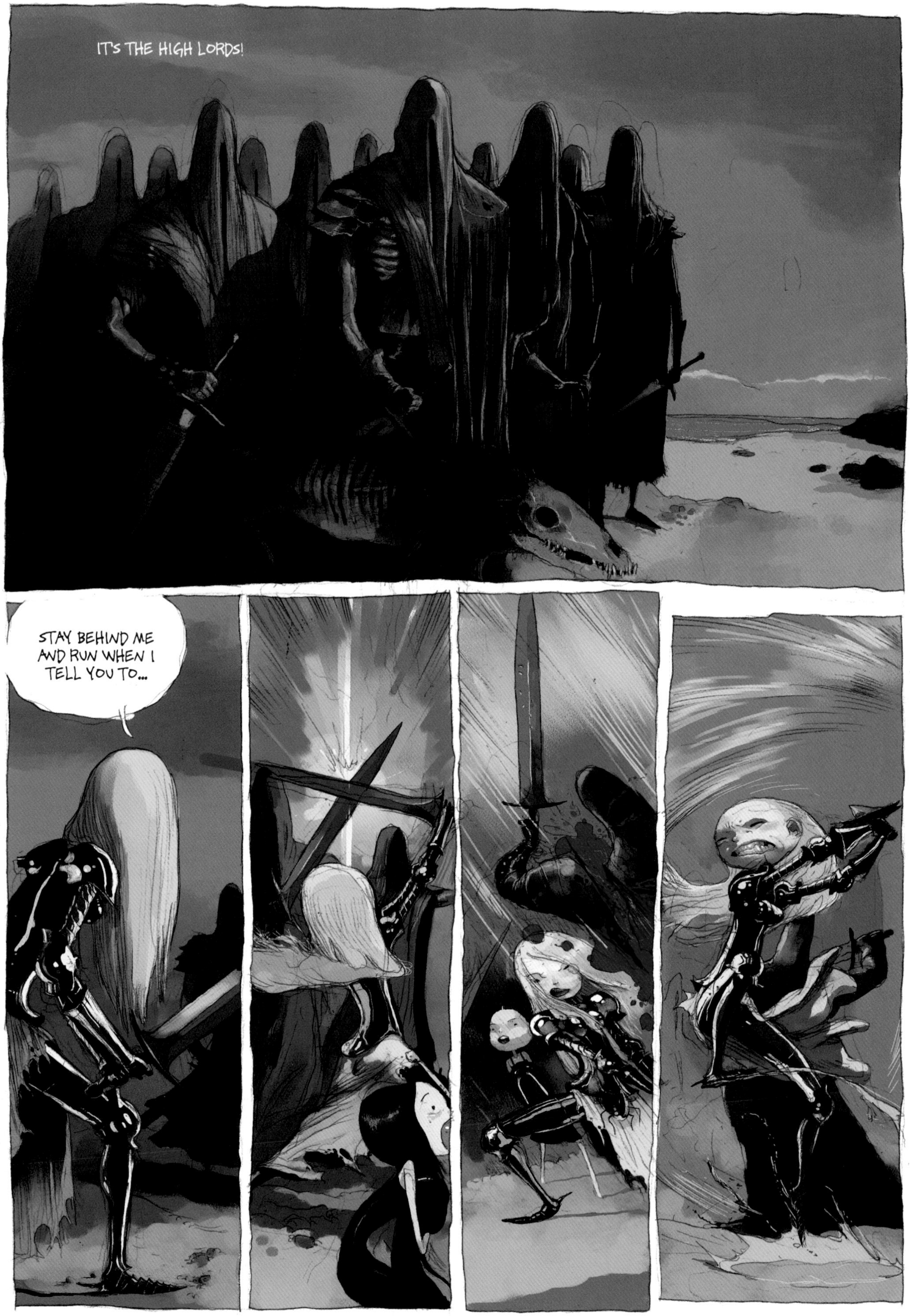

IT'S THE HIGH LORDS!

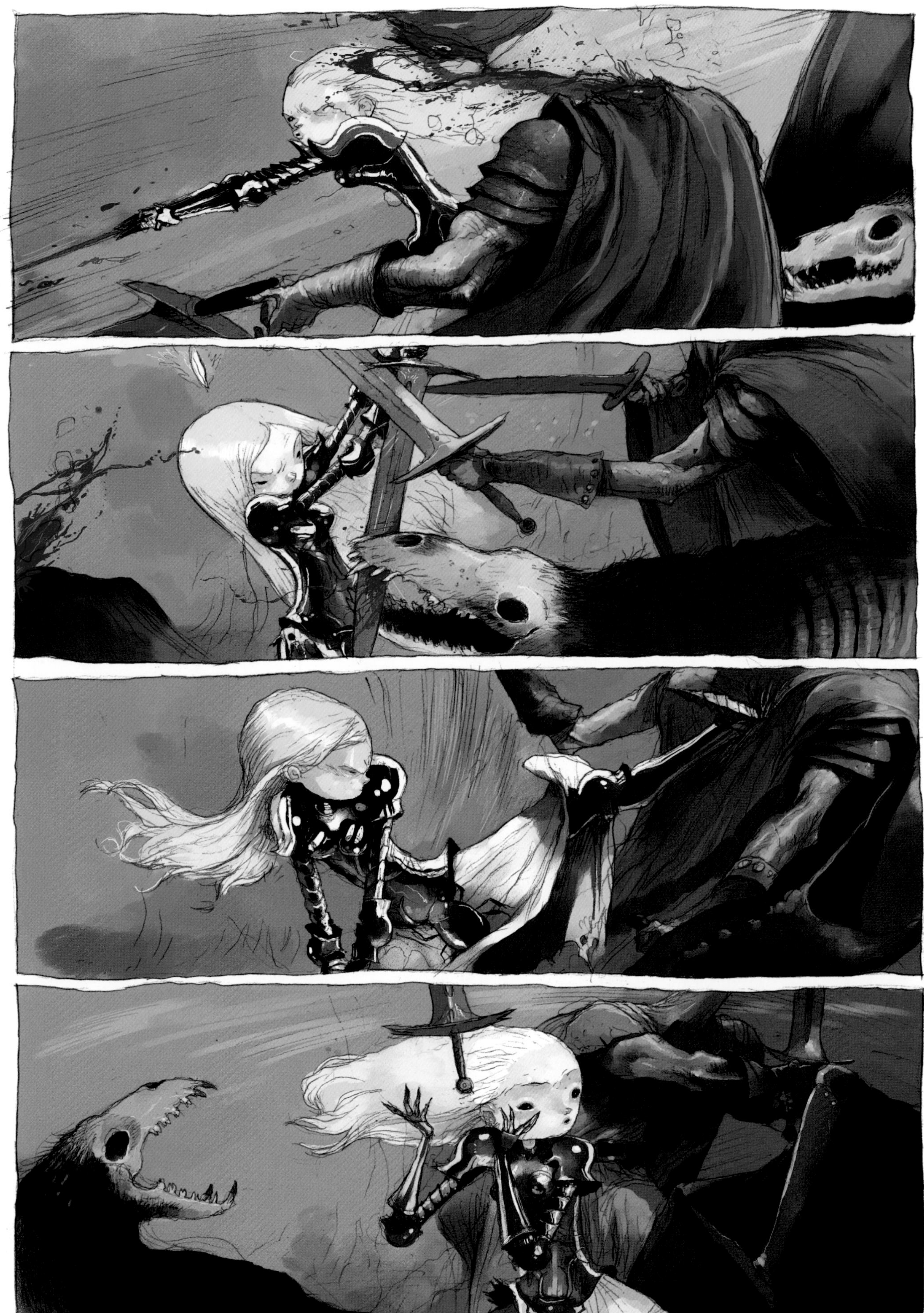

YOU BLEED TOO MUCH FOR A GHOST!

WE MAY BE DEAD, BUT WE ARE STILL FULL OF FURY!

THEN BLEED SOME MORE!

MILA! RUN!

OH SHIT OH SHIT OH SHIT

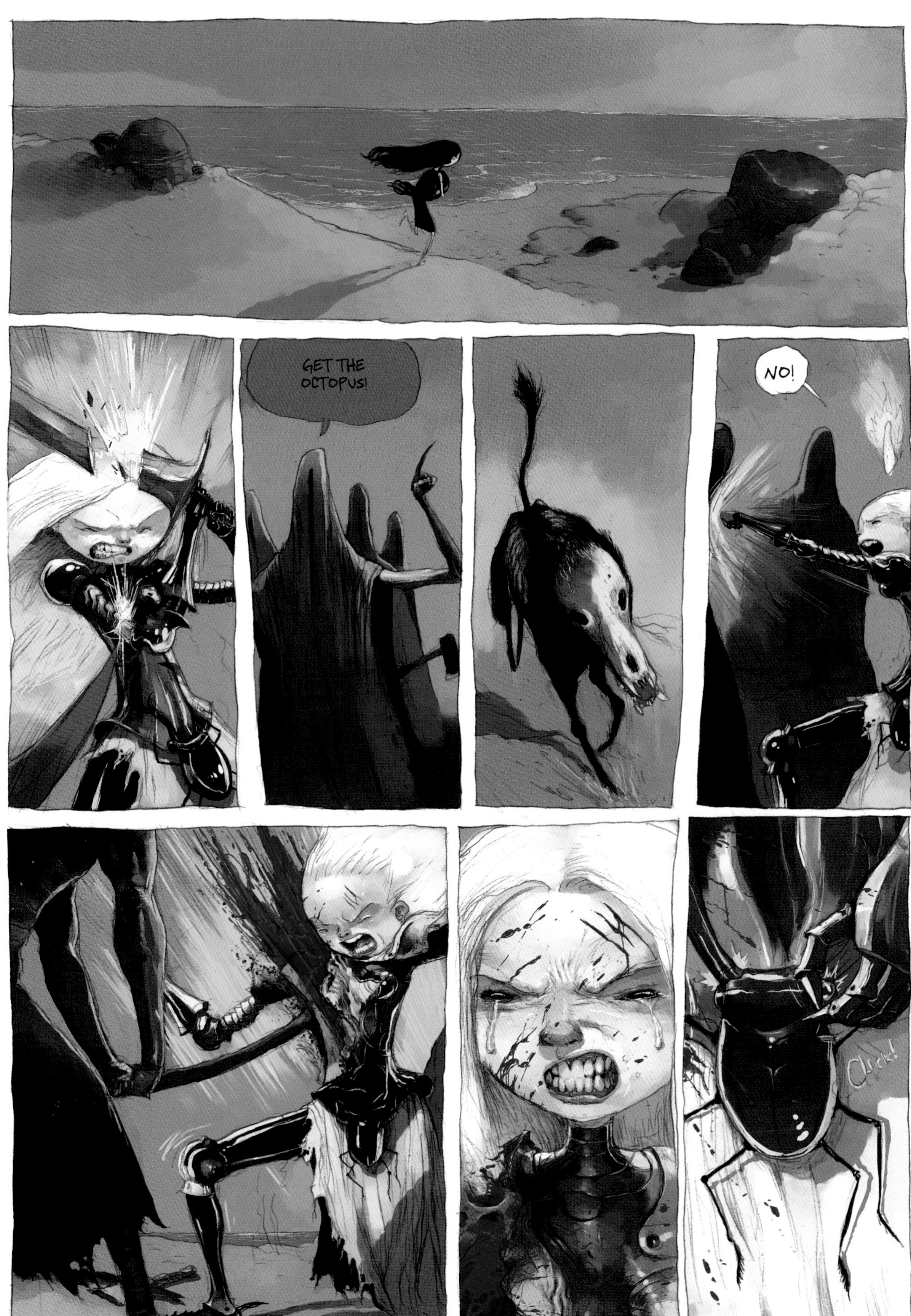
GET THE OCTOPUS!
NO!
Click!

Bzzzz

GET UP!
GET UP!
OW!
GRR
IT'S OVER!
LEAVE HIM ALONE!

AH!

YOU'RE NOT A COWARD AFTER ALL...
SHUT UP! IT STILL HURTS...

THE PAIN...
IT'S...

...TOO MUCH...

IS THIS...
??

WE DID ALL THIS FOR...

...NOTHING.

WE DIED...

...JUST LIKE THOSE DISTANT STARS.

CONDEMNED TO BECOME PART OF THESE FORGOTTEN RUINS...

TILL THE END OF EVERY DREAM...

EVERY TIDE...

EVERY WAVE...

...BUT WHAT IS THIS?

THE WATER!
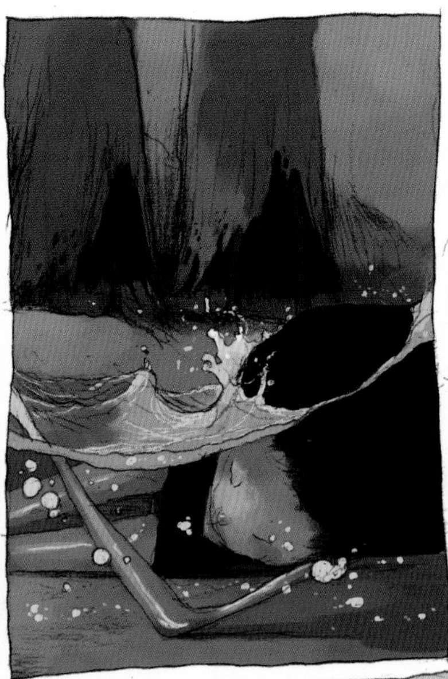

A TIDAL WAVE!

DID WE DO IT?

WE OFFER OUR THANKS.

YOU HAVE RETURNED OUR KING TO US.

WE COME FROM A DISTANT PAST...
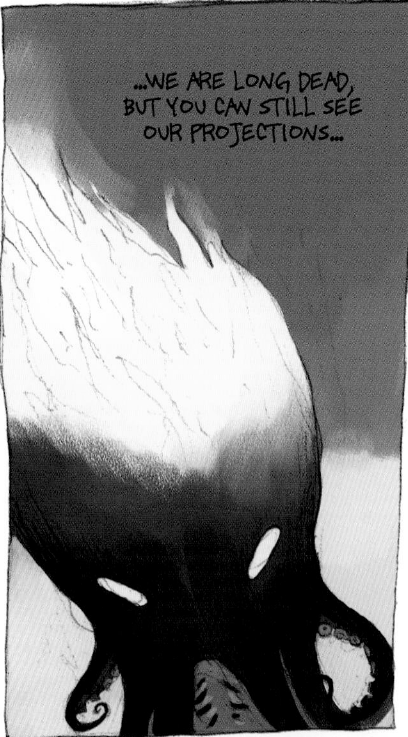
...WE ARE LONG DEAD, BUT YOU CAN STILL SEE OUR PROJECTIONS...
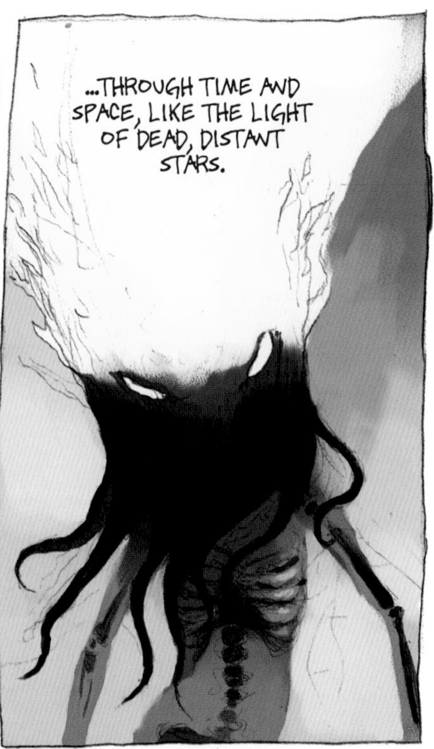
...THROUGH TIME AND SPACE, LIKE THE LIGHT OF DEAD, DISTANT STARS.

BUT WHEN THAT LIGHT PASSES THROUGH YOUR SOUL, IT BENDS...
...IT TRANSFORMS...

...ACCORDING TO YOUR MAGIC.

WOW... I DIDN'T THINK YOU'D BE SO... HOT!

SO WHEN I KISSED AGNES...
...I WAS REALLY KISSING YOU?

I DON'T FEEL PAIN ANYMORE...
THIS IS SOOO WEIRD...
WH...?! MY LEG! MY FOOT! THAT'S... WOW! I DON'T BELIEVE IT!
GOODBYE, BRAVE MILA!

OH NO! ANOTHER WAVE!

NOT AGAIN...

SPLASSHHH!

MM MMM

-GASP-

WHOA, WHAT A DREAM!

AGNES?!

HER TEETH...!
GAAAAH

...THEY'RE ALL THERE!
WHAT? -YAWN-

YOU WON'T BELIEVE THE DREAM I JUST HAD...
...AAAH!

THE OCTOPUS IS GONE!
YESSSS!

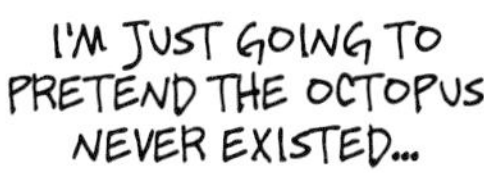
I'M JUST GOING TO PRETEND THE OCTOPUS NEVER EXISTED...

LOOK AT ALL THOSE RED FLOWERS! THEY WEREN'T HERE BEFORE!

I GUESS THEY BLOSSOMED OVERNIGHT... MAYBE IT RAINED...

YEAH! A RAIN OF BLOOD!

HM...

LET'S GO. WE'RE DONE HERE. WE CLEARLY DID SOMETHING TO CHANGE THINGS AROUND HERE...
WE SHOULD PROBABLY SNEAK OUT DISCRETELY.

I'M GONNA BE IN SO MUCH TROUBLE...
I'M SORRY, IT'S ALL MY FAULT...
IF YOUR PARENTS COULD SEE ME, I'D EXPLAIN, BUT...

IT'S FINE. I'LL BE GROUNDED FOR A YEAR, AT LEAST...
...BUT I PLAN ON SLEEPING FOR A WHOLE WEEK ANYWAY.

THERE'S JULIEN.
YEAH, HE'S AN EARLY BIRD.

OH, HEY, MILA. WHAT'RE YOU DOING HERE?
UH... HEY, JULIEN.
ARE YOU TWO HEADED FOR SCHOOL?
TWO?! YOU CAN...
...SEE ME...?
AGNES?!
...
...IS IT REALLY YOU?

YEAH, BUT... HOW IS THIS POSSIBLE?!
I... I CAN'T BELIEVE IT!

MOM!

MOM!

MOM!

I...

...I DON'T KNOW WHAT TO DO...!

GO.
GET IN THERE AND GO BACK TO YOUR FAMILY.

BUT... OKAY.

THAT WAS THE FIRST COLD MORNING OF THAT LATE AUTUMN...

THE WIND CURLED THROUGH HER HAIR AND CAPE IN A UNIQUE, ALMOST PLAYFUL WAY, AND ONLY FOR HER.

AND I JUST STOOD THERE...
ME, THE PRAGMATIC, THE COWARD!
WATCHING THE MOST DREAMLIKE
PERSON I'VE EVER MET FACE REALITY.

I WONDERED IF THIS WHOLE ADVENTURE WITH THE
OCTOPUS KING AND HIS ARMY OF WARRIOR TEETH
REALLY HAPPENED.

OR IF AGNES REALLY JUST RAN AWAY YEARS
AGO AND MADE THIS WHOLE THING UP.

EITHER WAY, THERE WAS CERTAINLY
MAGIC IN THE AIR THAT DAY.

WAIT... WHAT'S IN MY POCKET...?

SKETCHBOOK

Autumn Snakes
and the lost tooth

ghosts
are you to bite me one day?
cada vez son mas timidos

and after
making a
horrible plan

?
Tony Sandoval 2010

Illustration by Gabo Sandoval